Uptown Country
175 Charming Recipes with Flavor and Flair

Donald G. Lewis

Skyhorse Publishing

www.skyhorsepublishing.com

10 9 8 7 6 5 4 3 2 1

Library of Congress Cataloging-in-Publication Data

Lewis, Donald G.
Uptown country : 175 charming recipes with flavor and flair / Donald G. Lewis.
p. cm.
Includes bibliographical references and index.
ISBN 13: 978-1-60239-053-9 (pbk. : alk. paper)
ISBN 10: 1-60239-053-3 (pbk. : alk. paper)
1. Cookery. I. Title.
TX714.L488 2007
641.5--dc22   2007005320

Printed in the United States of America

Contents

Introduction

THIS COLLECTION OF OUR FAMILY'S recipes was inspired by my wonderful parents, Woodrow and Geraldine Lewis. They made a dramatic impact on my life, each for different reasons. From Mother, I learned how a wife with seven children could balance the needs of her family with the needs of her friends and neighbors. If someone she knew was short on food, sick, or had no money to buy new clothes, Mother made sure nobody went without. She also taught me an appreciation for good food, much of which was grown fresh in her large garden. She loved fresh vegetables like peas, tomatoes, and cantaloupes, canning and freezing healthy portions for our winter and spring meals. There was also an endless supply of homegrown fresh eggs that Mother made for breakfast and used in her cakes, which always came out tall, light and fluffy. As a child, my grandmother and I used to pick berries just in time for mother to make a special cobbler. There was always something wholesome to eat because of her hard work and dedication to her family.

Daddy was a man of few words but great action. He worked from early morning until dark, driving the tractor, working cattle, bailing hay. He always had time, though, for a game of dominoes, or a pecan picking run. He didn't have much of a formal education, though he realized the value in one, encouraging all of his children to study hard, as well as reading on the side when he had time. From him I learned not only how to get things done, but old fashioned virtues like dependability and hard work.

In a way, the name *Uptown Country* is a marriage of both of these attitudes: freshness and quality, along with a down-home simplicity. We celebrate the farm and all its bounty in our recipes as well as the freshness and quality of each of its ingredients. My greatest joy is for you and your family to bring the "country" back to your home with an "uptown" flair.

Appetizers

Cucumber Sandwiches

1	(8-ounce) package of cream cheese
2	tablespoons sour cream
2	teaspoons grated onion
¹/₄	teaspoon celery salt
1	medium cucumber, peeled, grated, drained on paper
1	towels
1	loaf wheat or white bread sliced thin

Place cream cheese, sour cream, onion, and celery salt in a food processor and process until smooth. Add drained cucumber and process only on and off. This filling may then be placed thinly on bread which will make 12 large sandwiches and may be cut into as many as 48 finger sandwiches.

Ham Ball

2	(4½-ounce) cans deviled ham
3	tablespoons chopped green olives
1	tablespoon prepared mustard
¼	teaspoon Tabasco Sauce
1	(3-ounce) soft cream cheese
2	teaspoons milk
1	cup dried parsley

In a large glass mixing bowl, combine deviled ham, olives, mustard, and Tabasco Sauce. Form into a ball or a log and chill for 20 minutes. Prepare frosting of cream cheese and milk and spread on ball. Garnish with parsley.

The Pickle Crock

Mother made sweet pickles each summer from the cucumbers in her garden. In their preparation, she used a large, white 8-gallon pottery crock. She would cover the cucumbers with lime and other spices, then let them soak in water for at least three days. When they were ready, she'd can the leftovers, which were usually enough to last the entire year. Of all her kitchen wares, the pickle crock was her prize.

Gruyere Cheese Puffs

1	cup water
6	tablespoons (³/4 stick) butter cut into small pieces
³/4	teaspoon salt
¹/4	teaspoon ground black pepper
¹/2	cup all purpose flour
1	tablespoon Dijon mustard
4	large eggs
1	cup (packed) coarsely grated Swiss cheese/gruyere

Position 1 rack in top third and 1 rack in bottom third of oven and preheat to 425. Butter and flour 2 large baking sheets. Combine 1 cup water, butter, salt, and pepper in heavy saucepan. Bring to boil over medium heat. Add flour and stir with wooden spoon until mixture forms over bottom of saucepan, about 2 minutes. Remove pan from heat. Beat in mustard. Beat in eggs 1 at a time. Beat in cheese.

Drop batter by heaping teaspoonfuls onto prepared sheets spaced about 1½ inches apart. Bake 15 minutes. Reverse position of sheets and bake until puffs are golden brown, about 5 minutes longer. Serve hot.

Crab Cakes with Herb Mayonnaise

	Vegetable oil spray
$^1/_2$	cup minced green onions
$^1/_2$	cup finely chopped celery
$^1/_4$	cup mayo
2	tablespoons minced fresh taragon
1	tablespoons Old Bay seasoning
1	tablespoons Dijon mustard
2	teaspoons lemon juice
2	teaspoons grated lemon peel
1	pound crabmeat, picked over
4	cups bread crumbs
2	large egg yolks
	Herb mayonnaise
	Fresh basil sprigs

Spray 2 baking sheets with nonstick spray. Mix green onion, celery, mayo, tarragon, Old Bay, Dijon, lemon juice, lemon peel. Stir in crab meat. Then add 1½ cups bread crumbs. Season with pepper. Stir in egg yolks. Place 2½ cups breadcrumbs in shallow bowl. Shape crab mixture into 1 inch patties. Coat with breadcrumbs. Fry in fresh oil.

Herb Mayonnaise

1	cup mayo
1/2	cup chopped green onions
1/4	cup parsley
1/4	cup gherkin pickles
2	tablespoons fresh lemon juice
1 1/2	tablespoons chopped fresh tarragon
1/2	teaspoon hot pepper sauce

Mix all ingredients in small bowl. Season with salt and pepper. Cover and refrigerate.

Vidalia Onion Cheese Dip

3	large Vidalia onions, coarsely chopped
2	tablespoons unsalted butter
1	cup mayo
8	ounces sharp cheddar cheese, shredded
1/2	teaspoon Tabasco
1	clove garlic, minced
	Homemade Tortilla Chips

Preheat oven to 375. Saute onions in butter. Blend with mayo, cheese, Tabasco, garlic. Pour into a buttered casserole and bake for 25 minutes.

Sweet and Spicy Mixed Nuts

¾	cup(1½ sticks) butter
¾	cup dark brown sugar
6	tablespoons water
1½	teaspoons salt
1	tablespoon Chinese five-spice powder
1	teaspoon cumin
½	teaspoon black pepper
½	teaspoon cayenne pepper
2	cups pecan halves
2	cups whole natural cashews
2	cups walnuts

Preheat oven to 350. Butter 2 rimmed baking sheets. Melt ¾ cup butter in large skillet. Add brown sugar, water, salt, powder, cumin, peppers. Add all nuts. Cook, stirring often, about 4 minutes. Divide nuts and syrup between the sheets. Single layer. Bake 15 minutes. Cool on sheets.

Savory Cheese Straws

1	pound frozen puff pastry, defrosted
2	egg whites, lightly beaten with 4 teaspoons water
2	cups plus 2 tablespoons Parmesan
¹/₂	cup finely chopped fresh herbs

Preheat oven to 400. Line the bottom of a baking sheet. Cut each pastry sheet in half. Keep chilled. On a floured surface, roll dough into a 10 x 12 inch rectangle. Brush with egg wash. Sprinkle with ½ cup cheese and 2 tablespoons herbs. Press into dough. Fold forming a 6 x 10 rect. Brush with egg wash. Turn the dough over and repeat. Slice folded dough with sharp knife. Place in freezer. Bake for 10 minutes, or until puffed and golden brown.

Parmesan Blue Cheese Toasts

	green onions
1	cup mayo
2	large garlic cloves, minced
1/2	teaspoon ground black pepper
1/8	teaspoon cayenne pepper
1 1/2	cups Parmesan cheese
3/4	cups blue cheese
28 1/3	inch thick slices from sourdough bread
	olive oil
3/4	cups finely chopped green onions

Combine mayo, garlic, pepper, cayenne in medium bowl and whisk to blend. Mix in cheeses, season with salt. Preheat oven to 350. Brush 1 side of each bread slice with oil. Place oiled side down on large rimmed baking sheet. Bake bread slices until almost golden, about 5 minutes. Spread 1 generous tablespoon of cheese mixture on each bread slice. Bake until cheese topping starts to bubble, about 10 minutes. Sprinkle with chopped green onions. Serve warm. Great with soup/salad.

Judy's Sweet and Sour Sausage Balls

My sister, Judy Lewis Groom, first introduced our family to this wonderful recipe. It has been one of our favorites and is welcomed by guests at any winter party. Prepare a double recipe as your company will enjoy these until they're gone.

2	pounds mild pork sausage
2	eggs well beaten
1	cup cracker crumbs
1/4	teaspoon salt
1	dash pepper
3/4	cup milk
1	cup water
2/3	cup catsup
1/2	teaspoon onion
4	tablespoons brown sugar
1	tablespoon granulated sugar
2	tablespoons vinegar
4	tablespoons soy sauce
1	cup vegetable oil

In a large non-metallic bowl, place sausage, eggs, cracker crumbs, salt, pepper, and milk. Mix these ingredients well. Chill for 1 hour. Form 1-inch balls and refrigerate. Fry in vegetable oil until brown and drain on paper towels. In a separate bowl, mix water, catsup, onion, sugars, vinegar, and soy sauce. Place the balls in a chafing dish or other suitable warming container and pour the sauce over them and saute for at least 20 minutes prior to serving. Enjoy!

Oyster Cracker Snacks

3	(12-ounce) packages oyster crackers
2	packages buttermilk ranch dressing mix
1	teaspoon lemon pepper
1	teaspoon garlic powder
1	tablespoon dill weed
2	cups vegetable oil

Place the crackers in a large plastic bowl with a firm, sealed lid. Mix remaining ingredients well and place over the crackers. Stir well. Replace lid and leave for 30 minutes. Invert container for 30 more minutes and serve when all the moisture is absorbed.

Farm Fresh Sausage

Daddy would take the leanest meat from our fattest hog and season it with spices, especially sage. He took great pride and precision in preparing our sausage, and it's a taste I haven't had since.

Puff Pastry Mushrooms

32	large firm mushrooms
¼	cup butter
1	(4½-ounce) can deviled ham
1½	teaspoons prepared mustard
1	package Pepperidge Farm Puff Pastry

Preheat oven to 425. Wash the mushrooms and pat dry. Remove the stems and set the caps aside. Saute the caps in butter until tender. Mix the ham and mustard and set aside. Thaw pastry for 20 minutes. Unfold thawed pastry onto wax paper. In each section of the pastry, place a mushroom cap and fill with the ham mixture. Fold pastry over making a turnover and cook until brown.

Beverages

Our Favorite Party Punch

1	quart can apple juice
1	quart can pineapple juice
1	quart can white grape juice
1	liter Sprite

Combine all juices and chill prior to use. Add ice or even crushed pineapple and 3 blended and mashed bananas for extra richness.

Hot Spiced Tea

2	cups apple juice or grape juice
2	cups pineapple juice
2	cups orange juice
$^{1}/_{2}$	cup lemon juice
4	cups strong tea
1	cup sugar
12	cloves
3	cinnamon sticks

Combine the juices in a large saucepan. Add the tea and the sugar and stir until the sugar is dissolved. Simmer the mixture after adding the cloves and cinnamon.

The Cinnamon Basket Chocolate Café Ole

1	tablespoon instant cocoa mix
$^1/_4$	teaspoon ground ginger
$^3/_8$	teaspoon ground cinnamon
1	cup hot house blend coffee
$^3/_4$	cup warm milk

Combine the cocoa mix, ginger, and cinnamon in a medium-size saucepan. Add coffee and milk and heat just until boiling.

Our Milk Cow

Jersey was like a member of our family. She was a large, black and white Holstein cow who gave rich, smooth milk that was a favorite in our home.

Mexican Hot Chocolate

2	cups hot fresh ground Colombian coffee
1	(1-ounce) square unsweetened chocolate
5	tablespoons granulated sugar
1	dash of salt
$^3/_4$	cup boiling water
$^1/_2$	cup milk
$^1/_2$	cup whipping cream
1	teaspoon vanilla
$^1/_2$	teaspoon nutmeg (optional)
$^1/_2$	teaspoon cinnamon (optional)

In a small saucepan, melt the chocolate over low heat. Add the sugar and salt and mix until well blended. Add the water and heat for 3–5 minutes. Combine milk and whipping cream and heat for 1 minute in the microwave or on the stove just until boiling point. Stir well the coffee, chocolate, and milk mixture until well blended. Add vanilla and garnish with cinnamon or nutmeg.

Salads

Favorite Tuna Salad

2	(6^1/$_2$ -ounce) cans tuna, drained
4	eggs
^{1}/$_4$	cup pecans, chopped
3	tablespoons sweet pickles, chopped
1	medium apple, cored and chopped
^{1}/$_2$	cup mayonnaise
2	tablespoons parsley

In a small saucepan, hard boil the eggs until done. Combine tuna, chopped eggs, pecans, pickles, apple, and mayonnaise. Serve on lettuce leaves. Garnish with parsley or chopped pecans. Yield: 6 servings.

Potato Bean Salad

4	cups potatoes, diced and cooked
1	(16-ounce) can garbanzo beans, drained
1	cup celery, chopped
¹/₂	cup green olives, chopped
2	tablespoons dried parsley flakes
2	teaspoons onion salt
¹/₄	teaspoon pepper
1	cup mayonnaise
4	eggs, hard boiled, sliced
1	teaspoon paprika

Combine diced potatoes, beans, celery, olives, parsley in a large bowl. Sprinkle onion salt and pepper. Stir in mayonnaise to coat mixture. Add eggs gently and stir. Chill thoroughly. Sprinkle with paprika for garnish. Yield: 8 servings.

My Garden

Only one time did I plant my own garden. For some reason, I planted English peas. Even in our Texas heat, they did reasonably well. One very special night, we had my English peas, Daddy's fresh pork tenderloin, ruby red tomatoes, and cantaloupes. With God's sun and rain, we were able to eat entirely off our own land.

Judy's Patio Potato Salad

$1/2$	cup milk
$1/3$	cup sugar
$1/4$	cup vinegar
1	tablespoon cornstarch
1	egg
$3/4$	teaspoon salt
$3/4$	teaspoon celery seed
$1/4$	teaspoon dry mustard
$1/4$	cup mayonnaise
$1/4$	cup onion, chopped
1	bell pepper, chopped
6	cups potatoes, diced, cooked

In a medium saucepan, combine milk, sugar, vinegar, cornstarch, egg, salt, celery seed, and mustard. Cook over low heat until thicker and well incorporated. Remove from heat. Blend in mayonnaise, onion, and bell pepper. Chill for 1 hour. Pour over 6 cups diced cooked potatoes. Mix well. Yield: 10 servings.

Cinnamon Basket Chicken Salad

Each Wednesday, our Cinnamon Basket Tea Room serves this chicken salad. People have enjoyed this special salad since we opened in 1988. During certain seasons, we have decorated it with violet leave or other edible flowers. You can use your leftover smoked turkey during the holidays for a lighter winter lunch.

2¹/₂	cups chicken, cold, diced
1	cup white and purple seedless grapes, cut in half
2	tablespoons parsley, minced
1	cup mayonnaise
1	cup whipping cream
1	teaspoon salt
¹/₂	teaspoon pepper
1	cup celery, chopping
¹/₂	cup pecans, chopped coarsely
1	teaspoon garlic powder
1	teaspoon lemon pepper

In a large non-metallic mixing bowl, combine chicken (or turkey), grapes, celery, parsley, and mayonnaise. Whip cream and add to the chicken mixture and add salt, pepper, garlic, and lemon pepper. Add pecans last and mix well. Garnish with extra parsley or finely chopped pecans, or grated cheddar cheese. Serve on lettuce leaf with our Country Banana Bread.

Strawberry Gelatin Salad

2	cups crushed pretzels (not too fine)
³/₄	cup butter, melted
3	teaspoons sugar
1	(8-ounce) cream cheese
1	cup sugar
1	(8-ounce) Cool Whip
1	(6-ounce) strawberry Jell-O
2	(10-ounce) frozen strawberries

Preheat oven. Mix and pour first three items into a 9 x 13 pan. Bake at 400 degrees for 8 minutes. (Do not overbake.) Mix the next three items and spread on cooled pretzels. Mix the last two ingredients lessening the water amount on the package somewhat. Add the two 10 cartons of strawberries and pour over cream cheese mixture. This delicious strawberry gelatin salad is served as an accompaniment to our chicken salad.

Raspberry Vinaigrette

¹/₃	cup raspberry preserves
¹/₄	cup vegetable oil
4	teaspoons rice vinegar
4	teaspoons cider vinegar
1	tablespoon dry white wine
1	teaspoon coarse mustard

Place preserves in medium bowl. Gradually whisk in oil. Stir in vinegar, wine, and mustard. Season with salt and pepper.

Parmesan, Pear, and Walnut Salad

1	tablespoon Dijon mustard
1	tablespoon dry sherry/red wine
1	tablespoon red wine vinegar
¼	cup olive oil
8	cups mixed baby greens
1	cup fresh Parmesan shavings
1	large firm pear, peeled, halved, cored, cut crosswise into thin slices
½	cup walnuts, toasted
1	shallot, peeled, thinly sliced

Whisk mustard, wine, red wine vinegar in medium bowl. Gradually add oil, whisking until well blended. Season dressing with salt and pepper. Toss greens, Parmesan, pear, walnuts, and shallot in large bowl to combine. Toss with dressing to coat.

Chunky Blue Cheese Dressing

1	cup crumpled Blue cheese, about 4½ ounces
1	cup sour cream
¼	cup mayo
2	tablespoons minced garlic
1	tablespoon red wine vinegar

Mix all ingredients in a bowl. Cover. Chill. Can use for up to one week.

Roasted Garlic and Bacon Dressing

¼	cup plus 3 tablespoons olive oil
½	cup peeled garlic cloves, about 12
4	bacon slices, chopped
¼	cup sherry wine vinegar
2	tablespoons minced shallot
1	tablespoon Dijon mustard
1½	teaspoons honey
1½	teaspoons mild molasses
¾	teaspoon dried tarragon
	Red onion, thinly sliced
	Blue cheese crumbled

Preheat oven to 375. Combine ¼ cup oil and garlic, cover with foil, and bake for 35 minutes. Finely chop garlic. Reserve roasted garlic oil. Cook bacon in skillet and drain on paper towels. Pour drippings into medium bowl. Add vinegar, shallot, mustard, honey, molasses, tarragon, and whisk to blend. Add roasted garlic, garlic oil, 3 tablespoons olive oil.

Soups

Creamy Onion Soup

2	thinly sliced medium onions
5	tablespoons flour
1	stick butter or margarine
4	cups half and half
1	dash of salt
4	cups beef broth
1	teaspoon Worcestershire Sauce

Saute onions with butter in a large heavy saucepan until tender. Add flour and beef broth and stir until smooth. Simmer for 5 minutes and add half and half, salt, and Worcestershire sauce. Simmer another 5–10 minutes. Yield: 6 servings.

Sausage Soup

2	pounds ground mild sausage
1	large onion, chopped
1	teaspoon salt
1	bay leaf
1	(16-ounce) can stewed tomatoes
1	teaspoon garlic powder
1	teaspoon basil
1	quart water

Brown sausage and onion in large heavy saucepan until onion is tender and the meat is done. Add garlic and season with salt and pepper. Add bay leaf, tomatoes, and basil and stir well. Gradually add the water and simmer until the soup is hot and the ingredients are incorporated. Yield: 8 servings.

Nacho Cheese Chowder

¹/₂	pound ground beef
1	(11-ounce) can condensed nacho cheese soup
1	medium tomato, chopped
1	teaspoon dried, minced onion
1	medium bell pepper, chopped
1¹/₂	cups evaporated milk
¹/₂	cup loose packaged frozen whole kernel corn.

In a large saucepan, place the ground beef, onion, and bell pepper. Cook until the meat is brown and the pepper is tender. Drain off excess fat. Stir in other ingredients and heat thoroughly. Serve with warm tortilla chips sprinkled with chili powder. Yield: 6 servings.

Broccoli Cheese Soup

1	large chopped onion
¹/₄	cup margarine
¹/₂	cup flour
2	quarts milk
2¹/₂	pounds frozen, chopped broccoli
3	pounds Velveeta cheese, cubed
3	cans canned sliced mushrooms

Saute chopped onion with margarine in a large heavy saucepan until tender. Add flour and gradually add the milk and cook, stirring constantly until the mixture boils and thickens. Add the remaining ingredients and stir to blend until the cheese is melted. Yield: 10 servings.

Potato Soup

4	cups peeled, cubed potatoes
1	cup finely chopped celery
1	cup diced onion
2	cups water
2	teaspoons salt
1	cup milk
1	cup whipping cream
3	tablespoons melted butter
1	tablespoon parsley
$^1/_2$	teaspoon caraway seeds
$^1/_8$	teaspoon pepper
$^1/_4$	teaspoon garlic powder
1	teaspoon Cavender's Greek Seasoning
1	cup evaporated milk

In a large soup or stew pot, add the potatoes, celery, onion, water, and salt and cook at medium heat for 20 minutes until the potatoes are done. Add the milk and cream and reduce heat. Add butter, parsley, caraway seeds, pepper, garlic and Cavenders. Simmer until ready to serve. If needed, thin with evaporated milk. Yield: 10 servings.

Creamy Tomato Soup

¹/₄	cup minced onion
3	tablespoons all-purpose flour
¹/₄	teaspoon pepper
4	cups tomato juice
3	tablespoons parsley
3	tablespoons margarine
³/₄	teaspoon salt
1	cup milk
1	bay leaf

In a large saucepan, add onion and margarine and saute until the onion is tender. Add flour, salt, and pepper. Reduce heat and stir well until smooth. Cook 1 minute. Gradually add milk and tomato juice. Cook over medium heat, stirring constantly until thick and bubbly. Add bay leaf and continue to simmer 1 minute at reduced heat. Remove the bay leaf and garnish with parsley. Yield: 6 servings.

Chicken Velvet Soup

1	large onion, chopped
²/₃	cup butter
12	cups chicken broth
2	cups heavy cream
	salt and pepper
1¹/₂	cups flour
2	cups milk
2	whole chickens
3	quarts water

In a large saucepan, place the chickens, onion, and water and boil until the chicken is fully cooked and tender. Remove chicken and strain the chicken broth and set aside. Remove the chicken from the bone and chop in small cubes. Set aside. Melt butter in a large soup container and add flour to make a paste. Gradually add broth and cook until thick and after 2 minutes, add milk and cream. Cook until thick. Finally, add the cooked chicken and salt and pepper to taste. Yield: 8 servings.

Corn Chowder

2	pounds Velveeta cheese, cubed
6	cups milk
4	bell peppers, chopped
	salt and pepper to taste
4	cans cream style corn
4	onions, chopped
1¹/₂	cups margarine

In a large saucepan, cook onion and bell peppers in butter until tender and soft. Cool. In another saucepan, heat cheese and milk and simmer over low heat until well blended and melted. Combine the corn and cheese mixture into the onions and simmer for 10 minutes. Season with salt and pepper. Yield: 10 servings.

Easy Stew

2	pounds stew meat
1	can cream of mushroom soup
1	package of dry onion soup mix
³/₄	cup red wine
1	(6-ounce) can potatoes
1	(2¹/₂-ounce) can whole mushrooms
1	(10-ounce) package frozen peas
2	bay leaves
1	cup vegetable oil
¹/₂	teaspoon salt
¹/₂	teaspoon pepper
¹/₂	teaspoon garlic powder
1	cup all-purpose flour

Sprinkle stew meat with salt, pepper, garlic, and dust with flour until well coated. Saute meat in oil until brown. Place meat in large soup or stew pot and add mushroom soup, onion mix, and wine and simmer for 10 minutes. Add the 2 bay leaves. Add potatoes, mushrooms, and peas, and simmer for 2 hours. Yield: 8 servings.

French Onion Soup

¹/₄	cup butter
2	tablespoons sugar
6–8	large onions, thinly sliced
4	cups beef broth
	grated Swiss cheese
	Deluxe Croutons

Saute onions and sugar in butter in a large saucepan until onions are soft and tender. Combine with beef stock and bring to low boil. Reduce heat and let mixture simmer. In each bowl, place croutons and cheese followed by the soup. Yield: 6 servings.

Deluxe Croutons

4	croissants, day-old if possible
¹/₄	cup butter, melted
¹/₂	cup Parmesan cheese
1	garlic clove
¹/₂	teaspoon garlic powder

Slice croissants in thin pieces and coat well with butter and sprinkle with cheese and garlic powder. Slice garlic clove in very thin slices and toss with coated croissants. Bake until brown in 350 degree oven for 10–15 minutes or until toasted.

Cream of Broccoli Soup

1	(10-ounce) package frozen chopped broccoli
¹/₂	cup onion, chopped
¹/₂	cup celery, finely chopped
¹/₄	cup flour
1	tablespoon margarine
1¹/₂	cup water
1¹/₂	cup milk
	salt and pepper to taste
2	chicken bouillon cubes
3	tablespoons parsley

Place broccoli, onion, celery, and bouillon in water and cook until tender. In another saucepan, combine milk, flour, and margarine and cook until a consistent paste is formed. Add this flour mixture into the vegetables and cook until thickened. Add salt and pepper to taste. Garnish with parsley. Yield: 6 servings.

Canadian Cheese Soup

1	large potato, diced and cubed
¹/₂	cup butter
1	cup onion, finely chopped
¹/₄	cup carrots, diced
¹/₄	cup celery, diced
2	(30-ounce) cans of chicken broth
¹/₂	cup milk
1	(10-ounce) package grated cheddar cheese
¹/₄	teaspoon salt
¹/₄	teaspoon pepper
2	tablespoons chopped parsley
1¹/₂	cup water
3	tablespoons flour
3	tablespoons cornstarch
¹/₂	cup old water

In a large covered saucepan, simmer the vegetables in 1¹/₂ cups water and cook until tender. In another bowl, combine flour, cornstarch, and cold water. When vegetables are tender, combine broth, milk, cheese, salt, pepper, and flour mixture and simmer for 20 minutes. Garnish with parsley. Yield: 10 servings.

Sausage and Rice Soup

4	cups cooked white rice
2	(10-ounce) cans rotel tomatoes
2	(15-ounce) cans ranch style beans
2	pounds mild sausage
2	medium onions, finely chopped
1	(8-ounce) can tomato sauce
1	teaspoon chili powder
	salt and pepper to taste

Cook sausage and onion in a large saucepan until brown and tender. Drain off excess fat and place contents in a large soup or stew pot. Add other ingredients and reserve 4 ounces of the tomato sauce to thin if needed. Yield: 8 servings.

Hearty Chicken and Rice Soup

6	cups chicken broth
2	cups cold water
¹/₂	cup uncooked rice
¹/₂	cup celery, sliced
¹/₂	cup carrots, sliced
³/₄	pound Velveeta cheese, cubed
1¹/₂	cups cooked, chopped chicken
1	(5-ounce) can drained mushrooms

In a large saucepan, cook chicken in 6 cups of water. Remove chicken and strain broth and set aside. Remove chicken from the bone and chop in small cubes and set aside. Combine broth, water, rice, celery, and carrots and simmer until the vegetables are tender. Add cubes of Velveeta cheese, chicken, and mushrooms. Continue to stir until cheese is melted and well incorporated. Reduce heat and simmer until ready to serve. Yield: 10 servings

Chicken Noodle Soup

6	cups chicken broth
1¹/₂	cups carrots, sliced
1	cup celery, sliced
¹/₂	cup onion, minced
1	(16-ounce) package egg noodles, cooked to directions
3	tablespoons parsley
1	whole chicken
	salt and pepper to taste
1	pinch of sage
1	bay leaf
3	chicken bouillon cubes
6	cups water

In a large saucepan, place chicken in water and boil until tender and fully cooked. Remove chicken and strain the broth and set aside. Remove chicken from the bone and chop into small cubes. In the strained chicken broth, add carrots, celery, onion. Simmer until the vegetables are tender. Add noodles followed by the chicken, parsley, salt and pepper. Then add the sage (if desred), bay leaf, and bouillon. Simmer over low heat until ready to serve. Yield: 10 servings.

Chicken Gumbo

cup water

tablespoons (³/₄ stick) butter cut into small pieces

teaspoon salt

teaspoon ground black pepper

cup all purpose flour

tablespoon Dijon mustard

large eggs

cup (packed) coarsely grated Swiss cheese/gruyere

In a large saucepan, place chicken in water and onion and boil until tender and fully cooked. Remove chicken and strain the chicken broth and set aside. Remove chicken from the bone and chop in small cubes. Set aside. In the chicken broth, add bell pepper and cook until tender, gradually adding chicken, bay leaves, tomatoes, and parsley. Add salt and pepper to taste. This is to be served over ¹/₂ cup white rice per serving. Yield: 10 servings.

The Chicken House

Not very far from our back door was a white chicken house with a fence around it. Each day we gathered large eggs for Mother's desserts. Those eggs were truly "golden" as her treats were made for royalty!

Creole Seafood Gumbo

1	cup onion, chopped
7	cups water
1	(10-ounce) package frozen sliced okra
1	cup sliced celery
$^1/_2$	cup uncooked regular white rice
1	(8-ounce) bottle clam juice
3	tablespoons all-purpose flour
1	teaspoon Worcestershire Sauce
1	teaspoon gumbo file or $^1/_2$ teaspoon dried whole thyme
1	pound fresh crab meat
1	teaspoon margarine
1	clove garlic, minced
1	pound shrimp, peeled and deveined
$^3/_4$	cup chopped green pepper
1	(16-ounce) can whole tomatoes, undrained and chopped
$^3/_4$	teaspoon salt
$^1/_4$	teaspoon pepper
$^1/_8$	teaspoon Tabasco hot sauce
1	(4-ounce) jar diced pimiento, drained
	Vegetable cooking spray

Coat a 5-quart Dutch oven with cooking spray. Add margarine and place over medium heat until margarine melts. Add onion and garlic and saute until tender. Add water, shrimp, okra, celery, green pepper, and rice and bring to a boil. Reduce heat and simmer uncovered for 30 minutes. Stir in tomatoes. Combine clam juice, flour, Worcestershire sauce, salt, gumbo file, pepper, and hot sauce. Add to gumbo mixture, stirring well. Cook over medium heat until mixture begins to thicken. Stir in crab meat and pimiento. Yield: 15 servings.

East Texas Stew

1½	pounds ground beef
½	cup margarine
2	cups potatoes, cubed
3	tablespoons chili powder
¾	cup onion, chopped
1	cup uncooked macaroni
2	(8-ounce) cans tomato sauce
1	(16-ounce) can cream style corn
3	cups water

In a large saucepan, combine ground beef and onion and cook until meat is brown and onion is tender. Drain off excess fat. Add potatoes, macaroni, and enough water to cook vegetables. Add tomato sauce, butter, chili powder. Simmer 15 minutes. Add corn last and simmer 10 minutes very slowly with low heat. Yield: 10 servings.

The Mebius' Gazpacho

In honor of my dear friends and adopted family, Jorge and Rosita Villa de Mebius from San Luis Potosi, Mexico, this recipe was developed and served at our 1990 reception welcoming them to our city of Athens, Texas.

4	cups tomato juice
$1/2$	cup cucumbers, finely chopped, unpeeled
$1/2$	cup tomatoes, chopped, unpeeled
$1/4$	onion, finely chopped
$1/4$	cup bell pepper, finely chopped
$1/4$	cup celery, finely chopped
$1/4$	cup diced pimiento
2	tablespoons wine vinegar
$1/2$	teaspoon salt
$1/4$	teaspoon pepper

Combine all ingredients and puree in food processor or blender. Cover and chill at least 3 hours. Stir before serving. Yield: 6 servings.

Squash Bisque

One of my good friends, Tere Williford, gave me this recipe for summer soup. It's wonderful!

3	tablespoons butter
1	cup onion, minced
1/4	cup carrots, minced
1/2	teaspoon salt
1/2	teaspoon pepper
2	medium potatoes, peeled and cubed
2	acorn squash, peeled and cubed
4	cups chicken broth
1/2	cup milk
1/2	cup heavy cream
1/4	teaspoon cayenne

In a large covered saucepan, saute onions and carrots in butter. Add salt and pepper. Add potatoes, squash, and chicken broth and cook until tender. Blend at low speed. Add milk and cream, then blend. Sprinkle with cayenne when served. Yield: 8 servings.

Carrot Soup

1	cup onion, thinly sliced
4	cups carrots, thinly sliced
6	tablespoons butter
1	teaspoon salt
$^1/_2$	teaspoon pepper
$^1/_2$	teaspoon thyme
4	cups chicken broth
4	cups water
1	cup rice
$^1/_2$	cup sour cream

In a large saucepan, cook onions and carrots in 4 tablespoons butter. Cover and steam for 10 minutes. Add salt, pepper, and thyme. Add broth and water. Heat to boiling and sprinkle in rice. Reduce heat and cover. Simmer 40 minutes. Stir in 2 tablespoons butter until melted. Serve with a dollop of sour cream. Yield: 8–12 servings.

Roasted Corn Chowder with Potatoes and Bacon

7	ears corn, husked
1	large red bell pepper
3	bacon slices, diced
1³/₄	cups onion
2	tablespoons butter
3	tablespoons flour
4¹/₂	cups chicken broth
2	large russet potatoes, peeled, diced
1¹/₂	cups half and half
2	tablespoons fresh chives

Grill corn until slightly charred and crisp-tender, about 15 minutes. Grill pepper until blackened and seal in paper bag. Let stand 10 minutes. Peel, seed, and chop pepper. Cut kernals from corn cobs. Saute bacon in heavy dutch oven, about 4 minutes. Add onion and butter. Saute until onion is soft and pale, about 10 minutes. Sprinkle in flour and stir 2 minutes. Gradually add stock. Add potatoes and simmer about 10 minutes. Stir in corn, pepper, and half and half. Simmer until chowder is slightly thick, about 20 minutes. Season with salt and pepper. Thin with more stock if needed. Garnish with chives.

Spicy Gazpacho

4	large tomatoes
3	cups hot and spicy vegetable juice
2	cups chopped seeded cucumber
1³/₄	cups chopped green bell pepper
1	cup chopped onion
¹/₄	cup olive oil
¹/₄	cup red wine vinegar
2	tablespoons fresh lemon juice
2	tablespoons Worcestershire sauce
	chopped fresh parsley

Bring large pot of water to boil. Add tomatoes. Blanch 15 seconds. Drain and cool. Peel, seed, and coarsely chop tomatoes. Transfer to large bowl. Add all remaining ingredients except parsley. Working in batches, blend mixture to coarse puree in blender. Season with salt and pepper. Cover and chill until cold, about 3 hours. Sprinkle with parsley and serve.

Vegetables

Corn Casserole

1	(no. 2) can cream style corn
1	(no. 2) can whole kernel corn, drained
1	large onion, chopped
1	medium bell pepper, chopped
1	small jar pimiento
²/₃	cup milk
2	eggs
1	cup cracker crumbs
1	cup grated American cheese
¹/₄	cup butter, melted
2	tablespoons sugar
¹/₂	teaspoon salt
¹/₂	teaspoon pepper
1	small can pitted ripe olives
	vegetable cooking spray

Preheat oven to 350 degrees. In a large mixing bowl, combine corn, chopped onion, bell pepper, pimiento, milk, eggs, crackers, cheese, butter, sugar, salt, pepper. Chop the olives and all at last. Mix well and place in well-sprayed 8 x 8 inch casserole dish. Cover and cook for 1 hour.

Marinated Vegetables

2	heads cauliflower
2	green bell peppers
2	pounds carrots
1	bunch celery
1	pound mushrooms
3	zucchini squash
1	bunch broccoli
2	medium cucumbers
½	cup salad oil
½	cup olive oil
3	cups tarragon vinegar
1	cup sugar
3	garlic cloves, minced
1	tablespoon salt
1	tablespoon dry mustard
	pepper to taste

Cut vegetables in bite-size pieces. Combine salad oil and remaining ingredients and mix well. Pour over vegetables and marinate well. Cover and chill at least 12 hours. Yield: 30 servings.

Twice–Baked Potatoes

2	large Idaho potatoes, scrubbed
4	strips bacon
¹/₄	cup green onions, chopped
2	tablespoons Parmesan cheese
¹/₂	cup sour cream
¹/₂	teaspoon salt
¹/₂	teaspoon pepper
3	tablespoons bacon grease
¹/₄	cup margarine

Bake potatoes wrapped in foil for 1 hour at 350 degrees. Fry bacon and drain off excess fat. Saute onion in bacon grease. Cut the potatoes in half and remove the contents and place in mixing bowl. Add cheese, sour cream, seasoning, and mash the potatoes well incorporating all ingredients. Add butter, bacon, and onion, stirring well. Add salt and pepper to taste. In the shells of the potatoes, add this filling and cook 15–20 minutes more at 350 degrees. Yield: 2 servings.

1015 Onion Pie

This is a fabulous addition to your steak dinner. The sweet 1015 onions make this an unusual compliment for a vegetable option.

2	cups herbed crouton crumbs
1/2	cup melted butter
3	cups sliced 1015 onions
3	tablespoons butter
2	eggs, beaten
1/2	cup milk
1/4	cup half and half
1/4	teaspoon nutmeg
1/2	teaspoon garlic powder
1/4	teaspoon salt
1/4	teaspoon pepper
	grated cheddar cheese

In a medium mixing bowl, combine bread crumbs and melted butter and make a crust for your pie plate. Briefly saute onions in butter and drain. Place onions in pie shell. In another bowl, mix eggs, milk, half and half, nutmeg, garlic powder, salt, and pepper. Top with cheddar cheese. Bake for 50 minutes at 350 degrees. Yield: 6 servings.

Squash Casserole

2	pounds yellow squash, sliced
³/₄	cup water
1	egg, slightly beaten
³/₄	cup cheddar cheese, gated
¹/₂	cup mayonnaise
¹/₄	cup bell pepper, finely chopped
¹/₄	cup butter or margarine
¹/₂	cup onion, chopped
¹/₂	cup pecans, chopped
2	teaspoons sugar
¹/₄	teaspoon salt
¹/₄	teaspoon pepper
¹/₂	cup plus 2 tablespoons cracker crumbs

Preheat oven to 350 degrees. Combine squash, onion, and water in saucepan. Bring to a boil and reduce heat and simmer for 5–10 minutes or until squash is tender. Drain and mash. Combine squash mixture with cheese, mayonnaise, bell pepper, butter, pecans, sugar, salt, pepper and ¹/₂ cracker crumbs. Use remaining cracker crumbs to sprinkle over casserole. Place in a greased cup 2-quart casserole dish and bake for 1 hour at 350 degrees.

Creamed Garlic Mushrooms

¹/₄	cup butter (½ stick)
10	ounce large mushrooms quartered
2	garlic cloves, finely chopped
1	tablespoon All purpose flour
1	cup milk
2	tablespoons whipping cream
1	tablespoon chopped fresh parsley

Melt butter in heavy skillet over medium high heat. Add mushrooms. Saute until deep golden, about 15 minutes. Add garlic and saute 30 seconds. Add 1 tablespoon flour toss to coat evenly. Add milk and cream and bring to boil, stirring constantly until thick, about 8 minutes. Season with salt and pepper. Mix in parsley. Serve hot.

Garlic Mashed Potatoes

4	pounds red skinned potatoes, peeled, cut into 1 inch
9	cubes
2	large garlic cloves
2	tablespoons butter
1	tablespoon fresh rosemary
¹/₂	cup canned low-salt chicken broth
¹/₂	cup Parmesan

Cook potatoes and garlic in large pot of boiling salted water about 30 minutes. Drain. Transfer potatoes to bowl. Beat with electric mixer. Add butter. Beat. Bring broth to simmer. Mix into potato mixture. Stir in Parmesan. Season with salt and pepper.

Roasted Herb Potato Medley

¹/₂	cup olive oil
¹/₂	cup balsamic vinegar
¹/₄	cup chopped shallots
2	teaspoon dried thyme
5	teaspoon chopped fresh rosemary
2	teaspoon fennel seeds, chopped
3	pounds medium-size red-skinned potatoes, cut into 8 wedges
3	pounds medium-size Yukon gold potatoes, cut into 8 wedges
	fresh thyme
	fresh rosemary

Preheat oven to 400. Oil 2 large baking sheets. Whisk first 6 ingredients in large bowl to blend. Add potatoes. Sprinkle with salt and pepper. Toss to coat. Using slotted spoon, transfer potatoes to prepared sheets, spreading in a single layer. Reserve oil mixture in bowl. Roast potatoes until tender and golden, about 1 hour. Return potatoes to reserved oil mixture in bowl. Toss. Transfer potatoes to baking sheet and rewarm if needed about 20 minutes. Garnish with fresh herb sprigs. Yield: 10 servings

Breads

Judy's Mexican Cornbread

Of all the recipes my sister, Judy Groom, has given me over the years, this one is the most valuable. We make it here at the Cinnamon Basket nearly every day and rarely have any left over.

2	cups cornmeal
2	cups flour
1	cup sugar
1/2	cup extra sugar
8	teaspoons baking powder
2/3	cup vegetable oil
4	eggs

(For plain cornbread, use the above recipe. It is great!)

2	pounds cheddar cheese, grated
1	pound bacon
2	medium onions, sliced
1	small jar of pimientos
1	tablespoon jalapeno peppers, sliced
2	teaspoons salt
2	cups milk
1	(16-ounce) can cream-style corn

In a large mixing bowl, place cornmeal, flour 1 1/2 cups sugar, baking powder, and mix well. Add oil, eggs, and mix until well blended. Set aside. Fry bacon and chop in fine pieces. Add bacon, cheese, onion, jalapenos, pimientos, salt, milk, and corn to the cornmeal batter and stir well. Preheat your well-oiled iron skillet in oven for at least 15 minutes. It is ready to use when it begins to smoke. Gently pour this mixture in and cook for 35–40 minutes at 350 degrees. Yield: 10 servings.

Pumpkin Bread

3¹/₃	cups sifted flour
3	cups sugar
1	teaspoon nutmeg
1	cup oil
2	teaspoons baking soda
1¹/₂	teaspoons salt
1	teaspoon cinnamon
4	eggs
2	cups canned pumpkin
¹/₂	cup pecans, chopped

Sift all dry ingredients into large bowl. Make well in dry ingredients and add all remaining items. Mix together until smooth. Portion into 3 bread loaf pans that have been greased and floured. Bake for 1 hour at 350 degrees. Cool slightly in pans and turn onto racks to finish cooling. Wrap in foil and store in refrigerator or freezer.

The Iron Skillet

The heaviest piece of cookware in our house was the well-seasoned black iron skillet. It was essential in baking the best cornbread you've ever had. We continue to use this 18-inch round treasure on a daily basis.

Apple Spice Muffins

¹/₄ cup butter
¹/₂ cup brown sugar
 1 teaspoon cinnamon
¹/₄ teaspoon ground allspice
 1 extra-large egg
 2 cups flour
 2 teaspoons baking powder
¹/₂ teaspoon baking soda
³/₄ cup milk
¹/₄ cup chopped apple

Topping
 2 tablespoons butter
¹/₂ cup brown sugar

Preheat oven to 350 degrees. Cream butter and sugar. Stir in spices and egg. In a separate bowl, combine flour, baking powder, and baking soda. Add to butter mixture, alternating with milk. Add chopped apple and stir well. For topping, melt butter and add brown sugar and place on muffin and bake 15 minutes.

Blueberry Muffins

8	tablespoons butter
³/₄	cup sugar
1	egg
1	teaspoon vanilla
1	cup milk
2¹/₂	cups flour
¹/₂	teaspoon salt
1	tablespoon baking powder
1¹/₂	cups fresh or frozen blueberries

Icing

1	cup powdered sugar
¹/₂	teaspoon vanilla
2	tablespoons milk
1	teaspoon lemon zest

In a medium-size mixing bowl, cream butter and sugar. Add egg, vanilla, and milk. In a separate bowl, sift flour, salt, baking powder. Fold wet ingredients into dry. Add blueberries gently. Bake at 350 degrees for 20–25 minutes in greased muffing tins.

For icing, combine in a small bowl and mix well. Glaze cooked muffins.

Banana Bread

2	cups sugar
1½	cups oil
3	eggs
4	bananas
3	cups flour
1	teaspoon cinnamon
1	teaspoon nutmeg
½	teaspoon salt
2	teaspoons soda
1	cup nuts, chopped

Preheat oven to 350 degrees. In a large mixing bowl, combine sugar and eggs. Add eggs 1 at a time, mixing well in between. Mash bananas in separate bowl and set aside. Sift together flour, cinnamon, nutmeg, salt, and soda in a separate bowl. Combine the sugar mixture, bananas, and flour until well-moistened. Add nuts. Cook in well-greased and floured loaf pans for 20 minutes or until toothpick inserted is clean.

Buttermilk Biscuits

2	cups flour
2	teaspoons sugar
2	teaspoons baking powder
1	teaspoon salt
¹/₂	teaspoon baking soda
¹/₃	cup shortening
²/₃	cup buttermilk
¹/₂	cup vegetable oil

In a large mixing bowl, sift flour, sugar, baking powder, salt, and soda. Cut in shortening until well blended. Add buttermilk, and form the dough using extra flour if needed. Roll out dough onto wax paper and cut into desired size. Place on oiled baking sheet and bake for 10–12 minutes in a 450-degree oven.

Grandmother's Butter

Churning was done every other day. The milk was strained into big gallon crocks and when the cream rose to the top, it was spooned off into a churn. It would take about an hour to get actual butter. Grandma would then take the butter paddle and work out all the milk, rinse it, and pack it in a butter mold. This fresh butter sold for five cents a pound, and of course it always sold out.

Cinnamon Raisin Walnut Bread

3^1/$_2$	cups unbleached flour
4	teaspoons granulated sugar
1^1/$_4$	tsp salt
2	teaspoons instant yeast
1^1/$_4$	tsp ground cinnamon
1	large egg
2	tablespoons shortening, melted or at room temp
^{1}/$_2$	cup whole milk at room temp
^{3}/$_4$	cup water at room temp
1^1/$_2$	cups raisins, rinsed and drained
1	cup chopped walnuts

Stir together the flour, sugar, salt, yeast, and cinnamon in a mixing bowl. Add egg, shortening, milk, water. Stir together with a paddle attachment until the ingredients come together and form a ball. Add just enough if the dough is too sticky or too dry and stiff. Sprinkle flour on a counter. Transfer the dough to counter and begin kneading. The dough should be soft and pliable. Knead by had for 10 minutes. Sprinkle in raisins and walnuts during the final two minutes of kneading. Lightly oil a large bowl and transfer the dough to the bowl rolling it to coat it with oil. Cover with plastic wrap. Ferment at room temp for approx 2 hours, or until the dough doubles in size. Divide into two equal pieces and form them into loaves. Place loaves into lightly oiled pans, mist the top with spray oil and cover loosely. Proof at room temp 60–90 minutes. Preheat oven to 350 degrees. Bake loaves for 20 minutes. Rotate the pan 180 degrees and continue baking for another 20–30 minutes. Breads should register 190 degrees. Immediately remove breads from their pans and cool for at least 1 hour (preferably 2 hours) before slicing or serving.

Focaccia Bread

5 cups unbleached bread flour
2 teaspoons salt
2 teaspoons instant yeast
6 tablespoons olive oil
2 cups water at room temp
herb oil

Stir together the flour, salt, and yeast in the bowl of an electric mixer. Add the oil and water and mix to form a wet, sticky ball. Work for 3–5 minutes or until dough is smooth. Sprinkle enough flour on the counter to make a bed for the dough. Transfer dough to bed of flour and dust liberally with flour. Coat your hands with flour and stretch the dough. Cover with plastic wrap. Let rest for 30 minutes. Stretch and fold dough again. Mist with oil, dust with flour, and cover. Repeat one more time. Allow the covered dough to ferment for 1 hour. Line a 17 x 12 inch sheet pan with parchment and pan the dough. Loosely cover pan with plastic wrap and refrigerate overnight. Let dough out for 3 hours before baking. Drizzle herb oil on surface and dimple it. Cook in oven at 500.

Herb Oil

Warm 2 cups of olive oil to about 100. Add 1 cup of chopped fresh herbs. Combine basil, parsley, oregano, rosemary, thyme, cilantro, and sage in any order. Add 1 tablespoon kosher salt, 1 teaspoon black pepper, 1 tablespoon granulated garlic.

Main Dishes

Italian Lasagna

$1/4$	pound lasagna noodles
2	tablespoons butter
$1/2$	cup onion, chopped
1	clove garlic, minced
$1/2$	pound ground beef
1	(6-ounce) can tomato paste
1	(16-ounce) can stewed tomatoes
1	teaspoon salt
$1/8$	teaspoon pepper
$1/4$	teaspoon basil
$1/4$	teaspoon oregano
1	(15-ounce) carton of ricotta cheese
$1/2$	pound mozzarella cheese, grated
$1/4$	cup grated Parmesan cheese
1	egg

Prepare noodles according to package. Saute the onion and garlic in butter. Add the ground beef and cook until brown. Add tomato paste, tomatoes, salt, pepper, basil, oregano, and saute slowly for 30 minutes. In a 9 x 13 greased baking dish, place 1 cup of tomato and meat mixture and spread evenly on the bottom of dish. Combine the egg with ricotta cheese. Place one layer of noodles over the sauce and add a thing layer of the ricotta mixture and sprinkle with mozzarella and Parmesan cheeses. Alternate the steps until completed. Prior to cooking, sprinkle the remaining Parmesan cheese liberally on top. Bake covered at 350 degrees for 35–40 minutes. Yield: 10 servings.

Fettuccine Alfredo

1	(12-ounce) package of fettuccine noodles
¹/₂	cup butter
1	cup whipped cream
³/₄	cup grated Parmesan cheese
¹/₈	teaspoon salt
¹/₈	teaspoon pepper

Cook noodles according to directions and drain. Melt butter and add cooked noodles. Add cream and cook slowly 3–4 minutes and add cheese stirring constantly. Yield: 4 servings.

Quick Spaghetti

1	pound ground beef
1	(6-ounce) can tomato paste
1	(16-ounce) can stewed tomatoes
3	cups water
1¹/₂	teaspoons chili powder
1	teaspoon garlic salt
1	teaspoon sugar
2	teaspoons onion, minced
1	(17-ounce) package spaghetti

In a large saucepan, brown the ground beef and onion. Add chili powder, garlic salt, and sugar. Add tomato paste, tomatoes, and water. Simmer for 30 minutes. Add spaghetti and simmer covered 30 minutes longer over low to medium heat. Yield: 10 servings

Chicken Enchiladas

1	whole chicken
6	cups water
1	(8-ounce) package Velveeta cheese, grated
1	cup onion, chopped
2	tablespoons garlic powder
20	corn tortillas
1	(10½-ounce) can cream of mushroom soup
1	(10½-ounce) can cream of chicken soup
1	(10½-ounce) can rotel tomatoes
1	tablespoon chili powder
1	teaspoon pepper

In a large saucepan, cook 1 chicken in water until done. Remove chicken and strain broth and set aside. Remove chicken from the bone and slice and sprinkle with pepper. Replace broth to saucepan and simmer. Moisten the tortillas in the broth one at a time and fill each with a selection of cheese and chicken. Sprinkle each with garlic powder. Roll up and put in greased baking dish. In another bowl, combine the soups and rotel tomatoes and spread over prepared enchiladas. Bake at 325 degrees for 45 minutes. Yield: 6 servings.

Martha's Meat Loaf

My sister-in-law, Martha Sloan Lewis, gave me this recipe over twenty years ago. It has been one of my favorites ever since. It is especially good with fresh cream, peas, fried okra, fresh tomatoes, and sliced cantaloupe. And of course, don't forget the cornbread!

2	pounds ground beef
1	(8-ounce) can tomato sauce
2	tablespoons brown sugar
1	tablespoon vinegar
1	teaspoon Worcestershire sauce
1/4	teaspoon salt
1/4	teaspoon chili powder
1/2	cup oatmeal
1/2	cup evaporated milk
1/2	cup onion, minced
	vegetable cooking spray

In a small saucepan, combine tomato sauce, brown sugar, vinegar, Worcestershire sauce, salt, and chili powder and cook until the sugar is dissolved and mixture has thickened. In a separate bowl, combine the ground beef, oatmeal, milk, and onion. Add 1/2 of the tomato mixture and stir the ingredients well. Form a loaf in the greased dish and pour the remaining sauce over the top. Cook covered for 1 1/2 hours at 350 degrees.

Mexican Luncheon

Of all the recipes in our cookbook, this is one of the most important for your collection. It serves many people, and when it is served with the cornbread, you will hear wonderful reviews for a long time. This is especially good on those cold winter days.

1	pound ground beef
1	pound mild sausage
1	cup onion, chopped
1	cup bell pepper, chopped
2	cups stewed tomatoes
1	(8-ounce) package spaghetti
1	cup buttermilk
2	tablespoons sugar
2	tablespoons chili powder
1	teaspoon salt

In a large saucepan, cook the ground beef, sausage, onion, and pepper until the meat is done and vegetables are tender. Drain off excess fat. Add tomatoes, broken spaghetti, buttermilk, sugar, chili powder, and salt. Cook uncovered for 10 minutes on medium heat and 20 minutes covered on very low heat. Yield: 10 servings.

Our Sack Lunch

When working out in the hayfield or clearing land, we anxiously awaited Mother's sack lunch: fried chicken, mashed potatoes, and other vegetables. A three-layer cake of fresh pie always came to our rescue. Those were the days!

Baked Chicken Breasts with Roast Garlic Sauce

6	chicken breasts, skinned and sliced
3	tablespoons dried rosemary
2	cups Italian dressing
2	tablespoons lemon pepper
1	head garlic, thinly sliced
5–6	mushrooms, sliced
¹/₂	cup onion, chopped
¹/₃	cup white wine
2	cups heavy cream

Marinate chicken breast for 6 hours in dressing, lemon pepper, and rosemary. Grill or bake in 350 degree oven for 45 minutes or until done.

Roast Garlic Sauce

In a small saucepan, place onion, mushrooms, minced garlic in ¹/₃ cup wine. Cook until the liquid is reduced by half at low temperature. Strain to remove vegetables. Add heavy cream and cook until thickened. Serve immediately over chicken breasts. Yield: 6 servings.

Winter Chicken and Rice

1	(6-ounce) package long grain and wild rice
1/4	cup butter
1/3	cup onion, chopped
1/3	cup flour
1	teaspoon salt
1/8	teaspoon black pepper
1	cup half and half
1	cup chicken broth
2	cups cubed, cooked chicken
1/3	cup diced pimiento
1/3	cup parsley, chopped fresh or dried
1/4	cup almonds, chopped, slivered

Cook contents on rice and seasoning packets according to package directions. While rice is cooking, melt butter in a large saucepan. Add onion and cook over low heat until tender. Stir in flour, salt, and pepper. Gradually add half and half and chicken broth. Cook stirring constantly until thickened. Stir in chicken, pimiento, parsley, almonds, and cooed rice. Pour in a greased 2 quart casserole. Bake, uncovered, in a 400 degree F oven for 30 minutes. Yield: 8 servings.

Southwestern Chicken

1	whole chicken
2	tablespoons butter
1	onion, chopped
1	clove garlic
1	(10½-ounce) can cream of chicken soup
1	(10½-ounce) can cream of mushroom soup
1	(10½-ounce) can rotel tomatoes, blended
1	teaspoon chili powder
⅛	teaspoon pepper
⅛	teaspoon salt
1	package corn tortillas
½	pound cheddar cheese, grated

In a large saucepan, boil chicken until done. Cut up chicken in slices. Saute onion, pepper, and garlic in butter. Add soups and rotel tomatoes. Add chili powder, salt, and pepper. Cut tortillas in small pieces and soften in chicken broth. Layer in a greased casserole dish, the tortillas, soup mixture, and chicken. Repeat. Sprinkle over the top cheddar cheese. Bake 350 degrees for 40 minutes. Yield: 6 servings.

Brisket Marinade

2	tablespoons Liquid Smoke
2	teaspoons celery seed
1	teaspoon onion salt
1	teaspoon garlic salt
2	teaspoons pepper
1	teaspoon slat
4	teaspoons Worcestershire sauce
1	cup water

In a medium bowl, mix the ingredients and pour over the brisket. Marinate overnight in a sealed container. Bake slowly at 250 degrees for 4–5 hours in a foil-covered pan.

Chicken Spaghetti

1	whole chicken
1	(8-ounce) package spaghetti
1	cup onion, chopped
1	cup celery, chopped
1	small jar pimiento, sliced or chopped
1	(10$\frac{1}{2}$-ounce) can cream of celery soup
1	(10$\frac{1}{2}$-ounce) can cream of tomato soup
1	(10$\frac{1}{2}$-ounce) can cream of chicken soup
$\frac{1}{2}$	pound Velveeta cheese, melted
1	tablespoon olive oil
$\frac{1}{2}$	teaspoon salt
$\frac{1}{2}$	teaspoon pepper
$\frac{1}{2}$	teaspoon garlic powder

In a large stew pot, cook chicken until tender. Remove liquid where chicken was cooked and strain broth. Cook spaghetti in the chicken broth while chicken is cooling. Drain spaghetti and add olive oil. In a large mixing bowl, combine spaghetti, onion, celery, pimiento, soups, and cheese. Add boned chicken and stir often. Season to taste with salt, pepper, and garlic powder. Place in well greased baking dish and cook for 20 minutes at 350 degrees. Yield: 10 servings.

Italian Chicken

4	tablespoons olive oil
4	tablespoons butter
3	medium onions, chopped
3	garlic cloves
2	medium bell peppers, chopped
2	tablespoons flour
1	(16-ounce) can Italian style tomatoes
1	cup chicken broth
1	cup dry white wine
½	teaspoon salt
½	teaspoon thyme
1	teaspoon sugar
2	tablespoons minced parsley
5	cups cooked chicken breasts
2	cups Parmesan cheese, grated
1	teaspoon Italian seasoning

In a large saucepan, heat olive oil and butter over medium heat. Add onion and garlic and cook about 5 minutes. Add bell peppers and cook 3 minutes more. Add the flour and stir in the tomatoes, wine, broth, salt, thyme, and sugar. Reduce heat and simmer for about 15 minutes. Add parsley and Italian seasoning and simmer 10 minutes. Place half of the sauce and chicken breasts in a shallow baking dish. Cover with remaining sauce and bake covered for 30 minutes at 350 degrees. Remove foil and bake uncovered 15 more minutes. Top with Parmesan cheese. Yield: 6 servings.

Quiches

The quiche, which is essentially a cheese pie, is a dish that has been around for years. It's very versatile and can be made easily and economically.

1	unbaked pie crust
1	medium onion, thinly sliced
2	tablespoons butter
2	cups Swiss cheese, grated
3	eggs, beaten
1	cup half and half
$\frac{1}{4}$	teaspoon dry mustard
1	teaspoon Cavender's Greek Seasoning
$\frac{1}{4}$	teaspoon pepper

Brown pie crust in 425 degree oven for 10 minutes. For flaky crust, put a cookie sheet under the crust. Saute onion in butter until tender. Place onion in pie shell. In a small bowl, beat eggs, milk, mustard, Cavender's, and pepper. Place cheese over onions and pour in egg mixture. Bake at 350 degrees for 45 minutes or until set. Yield: 8 servings.

In Search of a Name

One day, we were at a loss for a name for a special seafood quiche. A dear friend, Judi Bateman, and her daughter were having lunch and we gave them the task of finding the proper name for this wonderful new recipe. They came up with "Quiche-Me-Quick." It was an instant hit!

Bacon and Tomato Quiche

4	strips bacon, fried and chopped fine
1	tomato, finely chopped
1	teaspoon garlic salt
¹/₄	teaspoon chili powder
¹/₈	teaspoon paprika
¹/₄	teaspoon Lawry's seasoning salt

Follow the above recipe and add these ingredients with the onion and cheese. Bake at 350 degrees for 45 minutes. Yield: 8 servings.

Spinach Quiche

1	(16-ounce) package frozen spinach
4	tablespoons sour cream

Follow the basic recipe and add these ingredients to the onion and cheese. Bake at 350 degrees for 45 minutes or until set. Yield: 8 servings.

The Cinnamon Basket Mexican Quiche

2	cups cooked chicken, chopped in small pieces
¼	cup black olives, finely chopped
1	medium onion, chopped
2	tablespoons jalapeno peppers
½	cup sour cream
¼	teaspoon cumin
¼	teaspoon paprika
¼	teaspoon garlic powder
¼	teaspoon chili powder

Follow the basic recipe and add these ingredients to the onion. Substitute provolone or cheddar cheese for the Swiss cheese. Bake at 350 degrees for 45 minutes or until set. Yield: 8 servings.

Sausage Quiche

1	pound mild sausage, cooked and crumbled
1	teaspoon garlic powder
½	teaspoon paprika

Follow the basic recipe and add these ingredients to the onion and cheese. Bake at 350 degrees for 45 minutes or until set. Yield: 8 servings.

Taco Pizza

1	pound ground chuck
¹/₄	cup chili powder
	sun-dried tomatoes
1	small jar ripe olives, chopped
1	(16-ounce) can whole kernel corn
	Monterrey Jack cheese, grated
1	(pint) sour cream
3	tablespoons chili powder
1	tablespoon Tabasco
	pizza crusts (We use Bobili bread shells)

In a large saucepan, brown meat with ¹/₄ cup chili powder. In a large pizza crust, place drained meat. Top with tomatoes and olives and sprinkle with corn. In a small bowl, combine 3 tablespoons chili powder and Tabasco. Place on top of tomato mixture. Sprinkle with cheese and bake at 450 degrees for 20 minutes. Yield: 8 servings.

Baby Roma Tomato and Onion Pizza with Rosemary Pizza Dough

3	cups warm water
3	tablespoons sugar
3	packages dry yeast (6 teaspoons)
½	cup olive oil
5	teaspoons salt
9	cups all purpose flour

Combine 3 cups water, sugar in medium bowl. Sprinkle yeast over. Let stand until foamy, about 10 minutes. Add oil and salt. Mound 9 cups flour on work surface. Make a well in center and pour yeast mixture into well. Gradually knead until dough is smooth and elastic. Knead about 8 minutes. Oil large bowl. Add dough and turn to coat. Cover with plastic wrap. Let rise 1 hour. Punch down dough. Knead gently until smooth. Shape into 6 balls.

Topping

16	plum tomatoes sliced ¼ inch thick
3	small onions sliced thin
2	tablespoons fresh rosemary leaves
6	tablespoons extra-virgin olive oil

Preheat oven to 450. Sprinkle 3 large rimless baking sheets with flour/cornmeal. Roll out each dough ball to 12 inches. Scatter tomatoes, onions, rosemary, and basil onto each dough round. Drizzle with olive oil. Sprinkle with salt and pepper. Bake pizzas until crusts are golden brown, 15 minutes.

Mustard chicken

2	tablespoons butter
3	shallots (coarsely chopped)
4	teaspoons cracked black pepper
1	cup dry white wine
5	fresh sprigs of rosemary
5	fresh sprigs of thyme
2	cups chicken broth.
8	boneless chicken breasts
¼	cup Dijon mustard
1	tablespoon yellow mustard seeds

Melt 1 tablespoon butter in saucepan. Add shallots/onion to cook slightly. Add pepper, saute until brown. Add wine, bring to boil. Add rosemary and thyme sprigs and add chicken stock and cook for about 20 minutes to ¾ cup. Strain in saucepan. Sprinkle chicken with pepper. Cook or grill until cooked through. Preheat broiler. Brush chicken with mustard. Sprinkle with mustard seeds. Broil for 2 minutes. Bring sauce to simmer. Add 1 tablespoon butter and whisk until melted. Spoon sauce over chicken and serve with mashed potatoes.

Roast Pork with Apricot and Honey Mustard Glaze

1	cup apricot preserves
1/3	cup chopped seeded jalapeno chiles
1/2	cup red wine vinegar
1/4	cup Dijon mustard
2	tablespoons honey
2	garlic cloves, chopped
2	teaspoons chopped fresh rosemary
3/4	teaspoon salt
3/4	teaspoon pepper
1	5½-pound center cut pork rib roast

Preheat oven to 350. Whisk all ingredients except pork in saucepan to blend. Place roast on rack in roasting pain. Brush with ¾ cup apricot glaze. Roast pork until thermometer registers 145, about 2¼ hours. Transfer pork to platter. Tent with foil. Temp will rise to 150. Bring remaining glaze to boil. Cut pork into chops. Serve passing remaining glaze as sauce.

Desserts

Toasted Coconut Cake

1	cup buttermilk
2	eggs
1	teaspoon vinegar
2½	cups flour
1	teaspoon soda
1	cup vegetable oil
1	teaspoon vanilla
2	cups sugar
¾	cup coconut

In a large mixing bowl, combine buttermilk and eggs. Gradually add vinegar, flour, and soda. Fold in oil, vanilla, and sugar. Mix well. Add coconut and pour into (3) 8-inch cake pans. Bake for 25–30 minutes at 350 degrees. Cool on wire rack.

Frosting for Toasted Coconut Cake

1	(8-ounce) package cream cheese
1	teaspoon vanilla
1	stick margarine
1	(16-ounce) box powdered sugar
1	cup coconut
2	tablespoons margarine

In a small saucepan, place coconut and 2 tablespoons margarine and cook until coconut is brown. Remove from heat and set aside. In another bowl, combine cream cheese, vanilla, margarine, and gradually add powdered sugar. Thin with milk if needed. Frost cake and top with toasted coconut for garnish.

Crusty Coconut Pie

1	unbaked pie shell (See Donnie's Pie Crust Recipe)
1/2	cup milk
1 1/2	cups coconut
4	tablespoons butter
1	cup sugar
3	eggs
1	teaspoon vanilla

Pour milk over coconut and set aside. Cream butter and sugar and add eggs 1 at a time, beating in between. Add coconut mixture and vanilla and blend well. Pour into pie shell and bake for 40–45 minutes at 350 degrees or until brown.

The Smell of Christmas

Mother would make everything from fresh coconut cake, to fresh chocolate, or lemon meringue pies. Her homemade yeast rolls were rising on the cabinet, ready to bake. Daddy would always have parched peanuts to lure us out of the kitchen until Mother was ready. Mother enjoyed the holiday season the best because she was able to show her love for us with what she prepared.

Pineapple Cheesecake

2	(4-ounce) packages lemon Jell-O
1	cup hot water
1	can evaporated milk, chilled
1	cup sugar
1	teaspoon vanilla
1	(8-ounce) package cream cheese
2	cups graham cracker crumbs
1	stick margarine, melted
1	tablespoon powdered sugar
1	cup crushed pineapple

In a small bowl, combine graham cracker crumbs, margarine, and powdered sugar. Mix well. Form crust in a 9 x 13 glass dish. Set aside. Dissolve Jell-O in hot water and chill for 20 minutes. Beat chilled milk until it forms stiff peaks. Beat the syrupy Jell-O until foamy then beat in sugar and cream cheese. Fold in beaten milk. Fold in drained, crushed pineapple. Pour into prepared crust and chill 4 hours. Yield: 15 servings.

Vanilla Maple French Toast with Warm Berry Preserve

9	eggs
2¹/₄	cups whole milk
¹/₃	cup maple syrup
¹/₄	cup sugar
1¹/₂	teaspoon vanilla
³/₄	teaspoon salt
³/₄	inch thick bread
¹/₄	cup butter
	warm maple syrup
	warm berry preserves

Whisk eggs in medium bowl. Gradually whisk in milk. Add ¹/₃ cup maple syrup, sugar, vanilla, and salt. Whisk to blend. Divide custard between 2 13 x 9 x 2 glass baking dishes. Arrange bread slices in single layer in dishes. Let soak 10 minutes. Turn over, cover and refrigerate overnight. Heat griddle or heavy large skillet. Brush griddle with butter. Add soaked bread and cook until brown on bottom, about 4 minutes. Transfer to plates. Serve with syrup.

Warm Berry Preserves

1	pound bag frozen unsweetened strawberries
1	pound bag frozen unsweetened mixed berries
²/₃	cup red currant jelly
¹/₃	cup sugar

Mix all frozen berries, jelly, and sugar in large skillet. Let stand until berries thaw, about 2 hours. Stir until mixture thickens but is still chunky, about 7 minutes. Cover and chill. Rewarm over medium heat.

Almond Crescents

1	cup margarine
$^1/_2$	teaspoon almond extract
$^3/_4$	cup sifted powdered sugar
2	cups all-purpose flour
$^1/_2$	teaspoon salt
1	cup oats, uncooked
$^1/_2$	cup almonds, finely chopped
3	tablespoons powdered sugar

Preheat oven to 325 degrees. In a medium-size mixing bowl, beat margarine and almond extract until fluffy, gradually beating in $^3/_4$ cup powdered sugar. Add flour and salt and mix well. Stir in oats and almonds. Shape the dough to form crescents. Place on ungreased cookie sheet. Bake 15–18 minutes or until light golden brown. Sift remaining powdered sugar over warm crescents. Yield: 3 dozen.

Butterscotch Brownies

1	cup butter
2	teaspoons vanilla
2	tablespoons molasses
2¹/₂	cups brown sugar
4	eggs
2	cups flour
1¹/₂	cups pecans, chopped

In a medium mixing bowl, cream butter, vanilla, and molasses. Add sugar and beat well. Add eggs 1 at a time. Beat until smooth and light in color. Stir in flour and nuts. Place in a 9 x 13 greased cooking pan. Bake at 350 degrees for 30–35 minutes.

Banana Nut Cake

²/₃	cup shortening
2¹/₂	cups sifted cake flour
1	teaspoon soda
1²/₃	cups sugar
1	teaspoon salt
1¹/₄	teaspoon baking powder
1¹/₄	cups ripe bananas, mashed
²/₃	cup buttermilk
2	eggs
²/₃	cups walnuts, chopped

In a large mixing bowl, stir shortening to soften. Sift in cake flour, soda, sugar, salt, and baking powder. Add bananas, and ¹/₃ cup buttermilk. Mix until all the flour is dampened. Beat vigorously 2 minutes. Add remaining buttermilk and the eggs. Beat 2 minutes longer. Fold in nuts. Bake in 3 (8-inch) greased and floured round cake pans for 35 minutes at 350 degrees. Cool for 10 minutes before frosting.

Frosting

¹/₄	cup butter or margarine
1	(16-ounce) box powdered sugar
¹/₂	cup ripe bananas, mashed
1	teaspoon lemon juice
¹/₂	teaspoon vanilla

In a medium mixing bowl, cream butter and 1/2 of the sugar until smooth. Add mashed bananas, lemon juice, and vanilla. Add remaining sugar. Beat until smooth. Frost cake. Yield: 12 servings.

Banana Split Cake

2	cups vanilla wafer crumbs
1½	sticks margarine
2	tablespoons powdered sugar
2	cups powdered sugar
2	sticks margarine
2	eggs
5	ripe bananas, sliced lengthwise
2	(6-ounce) cans crushed pineapple, well drained
1	(16-ounce) carton dairy topping
½	cup pecans, chopped
1	small jar maraschino cherries

In a small bowl, combine the crumbs with the 1½ sticks margarine and 2 tablespoons powdered sugar. Press mixture into a 9 x 13 in pan for the crust. Set aside. In another bowl, combine powdered sugar, 2 sticks margarine, and eggs and beat for 10 minutes. Pour over crust and layer with bananas. Cover bananas with drained crushed pineapple. Top with dairy topping, and garnish with pecans and cherries. Refrigerate for at least 2 hours prior to serving. Yield: 12 servings.

Buttermilk Pie

2	cups sugar
3	tablespoons flour
1	cup buttermilk
½	cup margarine
3	eggs, beaten
1	teaspoon vanilla
½	teaspoon nutmeg
1	unbaked pie shell (See Donnie's Pie Crust)

In a medium-size bowl, cream sugar and margarine. Add flour and eggs. Beat well. Add buttermilk and vanilla. Bake at 350 degrees for 40–45 minutes in an unbaked pie shell. Garnish with nutmeg when completed.

Blueberry Tea Cake

1	egg
2/3	cup sugar
1 1/2	cups sifted cake flour
3	tablespoons margarine, melted
3/4	teaspoon salt
1/3	cup milk
2	teaspoons baking powder
2	tablespoons sugar
1	cup fresh blueberries
1/2	teaspoon cinnamon
2	tablespoons shortening
1	teaspoon vanilla

Preheat oven to 400 degree. Generously grease a 9 x 13 baking dish. In a medium-size bowl, beat the egg with a wooden spoon. Gradually add sugar, and mix until smooth. Sit together the flour, baking powder, cinnamon, and salt. Combine flour mixture with the egg mixture and add the milk gradually beating thoroughly after each addition. When batter is blended, add melted margarine and vanilla. Beat thoroughly. Add blueberries all at one time and gently fold into batter. Pour cake batter into prepared pan and sprinkle with 2 tablespoons sugar. Bake for 25 minutes. Yield: 8 servings.

Buttermilk Pralines

2   cups sugar
1   teaspoon soda
1   cup buttermilk
1   teaspoon vanilla
2   cups pecans

Combine the sugar, soda, and buttermilk in a heavy, large pan and cook over medium heat. The candy thermometer should read at least 234 degrees. Remove from heat and add vanilla and 2 cups pecans. Begin beating immediately. Beat until candy thickens slightly. Beating by hand is preferred. Drop a teaspoon amount onto waxed paper. Cool. Thin with a few drops of warm water if needed. Yield: 30 pralines.

Carrot Cake

1	cup whole wheat flour
2	teaspoons ground cinnamon
½	teaspoon salt
½	cup sweet butter
½	cup vegetable oil
2	teaspoons vanilla extract
1	grated rind of 1 lemon
½	cup golden raisins
1	cup all-purpose flour
1	teaspoon ground nutmeg
1½	teaspoon baking soda
2	cups sugar
4	extra-large eggs
1	pound carrots, coarsely grated

Preheat oven to 350 degrees. Grease and flour 2 (9-inch) round cake pans. Combine the flours, cinnamon, nutmeg, salt, and baking soda in a mixing bowl. In a separate bowl, cream the butter and sugar with a hand beater until light and fluffy. Add the oil and mix well. Add the eggs 1 at a time, beating well after each addition. Stir in the vanilla extract. Fold in the dry ingredients, then the carrots, raisins, and lemon rind. Divide the batter between the pans. Bake 25–30 minutes. Frost top of each layer with Cream Cheese Frosting.

Cream Cheese Frosting

1	pound cream cheese, room temperature
³/₄	cup butter, room temperature
4	cups unsifted powdered sugar
1	teaspoon vanilla extract
1	teaspoon freshly squeezed lemon juice

In a small saucepan, place coconut and 2 tablespoons margarine and cook until coconut is brown. Remove from heat and set aside. In another bowl, combine cream cheese, vanilla, margarine, and gradually add powdered sugar. Thin with milk if needed. Frost cake and top with toasted coconut for garnish.

Caramel Oatmeal Bars

1³/₄	cups oats, uncooked
1¹/₂	cups all-purpose flour
³/₄	cup brown sugar, firmly packed
¹/₂	teaspoon baking soda
¹/₄	teaspoon salt
³/₄	cup margarine, melted
1	(14-ounce) vanilla caramels
¹/₄	cup water
1	cup pecans, chopped
1	(6-ounce) package semi-sweet chocolate chips

Preheat oven to 350 degrees. Grease a 9 x 13 baking dish. Combine oats, flour, brown sugar, baking soda, and salt. Add margarine, mixing until crumbly. Reserve 1 cup of oats mixture for topping. Press remaining onto bottom of prepared pan. Bake 10 minutes. In a small saucepan, combine caramels and water. Melt over low heat, stirring until caramels are melted and mixture is smooth. Sprinkle chocolate and nuts over the oatmeal crust. Drizzle caramel mixture over the chocolate/nuts. Sprinkle reserved oatmeal mixture on top and bake for 15–18 minutes until light golden brown. Cool completely. Chill until chocolate is set. Cut into 2-inch bars. Store tightly. Yield: 12 squares.

Coconut Toffee Bars

¹/₂	cup brown sugar plus 1 cup
¹/₄	cup margarine
¹/₄	cup shortening
1	cup flour plus 2 tablespoons
2	eggs
1	teaspoon baking powder
¹/₂	teaspoon salt
1	cup coconut
1	cup pecans, chopped
1	teaspoon vanilla

Preheat oven to 350 degrees. In a medium-size mixing bowl, combine ¹/₂ cup brown sugar, ¹/₄ cup margarine, shortening, and 1 cup flour. Press into a 9 x 13 baking pan for the crust. Bake 10 minutes. In a larger mixing bowl, beat eggs and gradually stir in 1 cup brown sugar, 2 tablespoons flour, baking powder, and salt. Stir in coconut, pecans, and vanilla. Spread on baked crust and bake for 25 minutes or until golden brown. Yield: 12 squares.

Company Cheesecake

1¼	cups graham cracker crumbs
2	tablespoons sugar
3	tablespoons margarine, melted
2	(8-ounce) packages plus 1 (3-ounce) package cream cheese
1	cup sugar
2	teaspoons grated lemon peel
½	teaspoon vanilla
3	eggs
	cherry glaze

Preheat oven to 350 degrees. Mix cracker crumbs, sugar, and margarine. Press into bottom of a 9-inch springform pan. Bake 10 minutes. Cool. Reduce oven temperature to 300 degrees. In a medium mixing bowl, beat cream cheese. Add 1 cup sugar gradually, and beat until fluffy. Add lemon peel and vanilla. Beat in 1 egg at a time. Pour over crust and bake until center is firm, about 1 hour. Turn oven off and let cheesecake remain all night to cool. Refrigerate at least 3 hours. Top with the cherry glaze.

Cherry Glaze

1	(16-ounce) can pitted red cherries
¹/₂	cup sugar
2	tablespoons cornstarch
4	drops red food color
1	teaspoon almond extract

Drain cherries and add enough water to make 1 cup. Mix sugar and cornstarch in saucepan. Stir in cherry liquid and cook, stirring constantly until mixture thickens and boils. Boil and stir 1 minute. Remove from heat and stir in cherries, food color, and almond extract. Cool completely and glaze cheesecake. Yield: 8 servings.

Coconut Raisin Bars

¹/₂	cup butter
¹/₂	cup confectioners sugar
1	teaspoon vanilla
1	cup, plus 2 tablespoons, all-purpose flour
1	teaspoon baking powder
2²/₃	cups (7-ounce) coconut
²/₃	cup raisins
¹/₂	cup semi-sweet chocolate chips
2	eggs

In a large mixing bowl, beat butter until light and fluffy. Gradually beat in sugar and 1 cup flour with ²/₃ cup coconut. Mix well. Press into an ungreased 9-inch square pan and bake at 350 degrees for 20 minutes. In another bowl, beat eggs and vanilla. Gradually beat in brown sugar. Stir in 2 tablespoons flour and baking powder. Stir in raisins and 1 cup of the coconut. Pour over crust in pan and bake 30 minutes. Sprinkle with the chocolate chips while the cake is still hot. Carefully spread to frost. Sprinkle with remaining coconut. Cool and cut into bars. Yield: 20 bars.

Chocolate Cinnamon Cake

On Saturday, we make this cake. It is one of our most popular and happens to be the easiest cake we prepare. Since we're called the Cinnamon Basket, this cake is our house dessert.

2	cups sugar
2	cups flour
1	stick butter
1	cup water
½	cup oil
4	tablespoons cocoa
½	cup buttermilk
2	eggs, slightly beaten
1	teaspoon soda
1	teaspoon cinnamon
1	teaspoon vanilla

In a medium-size bowl mixing bowl, sift sugar and flour. Combine in a saucepan: butter, water, oil, and cocoa. Bring to a boil. Pour over dry ingredients. In another bowl, add buttermilk, egg, soda, cinnamon, and vanilla. Beat 2 minutes and add to other ingredients. Bake in a 9 x 13 greased glass pan for 35 minutes at 350 degrees. Yield: 15 pieces.

Chocolate Cinnamon Cake Icing

1	stick butter
6	tablespoons milk
4	tablespoons cocoa
1	(16-ounce) box confectioners' sugar
1	cup nuts, chopped
1	teaspoon vanilla

Chocolate Fudge Cake

2	cups cake flour
2	cups sugar
1	stick butter
4	tablespoons cocoa
1/2	cup shortening
1	cup water
1/2	cup buttermilk
1	teaspoon soda
1	teaspoon vanilla
2	eggs

In a medium mixing bowl, combine cake flour and sugar. Set aside. In a saucepan, bring butter, cocoa, shortening, and water to a boil. Combine flour mixture with liquid mixture. Add buttermilk, soda, vanilla, and eggs, and beat until smooth. Pour into greased and floured 9 x 11-inch pan. Bake at 350 degrees for 25 minutes. Frost with the following:

Chocolate Fudge Icing

1	stick butter
4	tablespoons cocoa
6	tablespoons milk
1	(16-ounce) box powdered sugar
1	cup coconut
1	cup pecans, chopped
1	teaspoon vanilla

In a medium mixing bowl, combine butter, cocoa, and milk. Add sugar and mix well. Stir in coconut, pecans, and vanilla, and combine well. Frost cake while it is just out of the oven. Yield: 15 servings.

Chocolate Nut Bars

1	(16-ounce) package semi-sweet chocolate chips
2	(1-ounce) squares unsweetened chocolate
2	tablespoons margarine
2/3	cup sugar
2	eggs
1	teaspoon vanilla
1/4	cup all-purpose flour
1/4	teaspoon baking powder
1/8	teaspoon salt
1	cup pecans, chopped
2	ounces white baking chocolate, chopped
1	(16-ounce) box confectioners' sugar

In a medium saucepan, heat dark chocolates and margarine over low heat until melted, stirring constantly. Remove from heat, cooling 10 minutes. Stir in sugar. Add eggs and vanilla, and beat by hand until combined. Stir in flour, baking powder, and salt. Fold in pecans and white chocolate pieces. Spread batter in a greased 9 x 9-inch baking pan. Bake for 30 minutes at 350 degrees. Sift the sugar for topping. Cut into bars. Yield: 24 bars.

Chocolate Oatmeal Bars

1	cup unsifted flour
1	cup instant oats
$^3/_4$	cup brown sugar, firmly packed
$^1/_2$	cup butter, softened
1	(14-ounce) can sweetened condensed milk
1	cup pecans, chopped
1	cup semi-sweet chocolate chips

Preheat oven to 350 degrees. In a medium mixing bowl, combine flour, oats, brown sugar, and butter. Mix well. Reserve $^1/_2$ cup of this mixture. Pour remaining on bottom of a 9 x 13-inch baking pan. Bake 10 minutes. Pour milk evenly over crust. Sprinkle with nuts and chocolate. Top with reserved oat mixture. Bake 25–30 minutes. Cool. Yield: 12 servings.

Chocolate Peanut Butter Cookies

2¹/₄	cups all-purpose flour
¹/₃	cup cocoa
1	teaspoon baking powder
¹/₂	teaspoon salt
1	cup butter
³/₄	cup smooth peanut butter
³/₄	cup brown sugar
³/₄	cup granulated sugar
1	teaspoon sugar
2	large eggs
5	(2-ounce) packages peanut butter cups, each cup cut into 8 pieces
1	(6-ounce) package semi-sweet chocolate chips

Preheat oven to 350 degrees. In a medium-size bowl, combine flour, cocoa, baking powder, and salt. Set aside. In a larger bowl, mix at medium speed the butter, peanut butter, brown sugar, granulated sugar, and vanilla for 3 minutes. Add eggs 1 at a time and beat thoroughly after each addition. Reduce speed to low, and gradually beat in flour mixture until smooth. Stir peanut butter cup pieces and chocolate chips into dough. Drop about 3 table-spoons per cookie onto an ungreased cookie sheet, spacing about 1 inch apart. Bake 13 minutes until the cookie is slightly firm to touch. Yield: 24 cookies.

Cream Cheese Brownies

This is another wonderful recipe my sister, Judy, gave me when I wanted to serve a large group and wanted it to be extra special. These are very rich, so cut them small and put them in the smallest pastry cups.

2	(4-ounce) packages German chocolate
6	tablespoons butter plus 4 tablespoons
2	(3-ounce) packages cream cheese
2	cups sugar
6	eggs
1	cup unsifted flour plus 2 tablespoons
3	teaspoons vanilla
1/2	teaspoon almond extract
1/2	teaspoon salt
1	teaspoon baking powder
1	cup pecans, chopped

Preheat oven to 350 degrees. In a small heavy saucepan, melt the chocolate and 6 tablespoons butter. Stir well and cool. Set aside. In a medium mixing bowl, blend cream cheese, 4 tablespoons butter, and 1/2 cup sugar. Add to this 2 eggs, 2 tablespoons flour, and 1 teaspoon vanilla. Mix well and set aside. In another mixing bowl, beat 4 eggs until light colored. Slowly add 1 1/2 cups sugar. Beat until thickened. Add baking powder, salt, and 1 cup flour. Blend in chocolate mixture, adding 2 teaspoons vanilla, almond extract, and nuts. To bake, spread half of the chocolate batter in a greased and floured 10 x 15-inch cookie sheet with edges. Top with cheese mixture. Spoon remaining chocolate batter over top. Zigzag knife through batter to marble. Bake for 35 minutes and cool.

Icing for Cream Cheese Brownies

1	stick margarine
5	tablespoons cocoa
1	teaspoon vanilla
¹/₃	cup milk
1	(16-ounce) box of powdered sugar

In a medium saucepan, melt butter and cocoa. Add milk gradually and barely heat. Pour over sugar and beat until smooth. Add vanilla and mix well. Cover entire surface with icing and garnish with pecan if desired. Yield: 96 1-inch squares.

Datenut Bars

2	cups flour
$^3/_4$	teaspoon soda
$^1/_2$	teaspoon salt
$^1/_4$	teaspoon nutmeg
$^1/_2$	cup sugar
$^1/_2$	cup molasses
1	teaspoon cinnamon
$^3/_4$	teaspoon baking powder
$^1/_2$	teaspoon allspice
$^1/_2$	cup butter, at room temperature
1	cup dates, chopped, pitted
1	cup pecans, coarsely chopped

In a medium mixing bowl, cream butter and sugar. Mix in eggs one at a time. Beat for 2 minutes. Mix in molasses. On low speed, add flour, soda, salt, nutmeg, cinnamon, baking powder, and allspice. Fold in dates and nuts. Bake in a 350 degree oven for 20 minutes in a 9 x 13-inch baking pan. Glaze with the following Lemon Glaze.

Lemon Glaze

$1^1/_2$	cups powdered sugar
1	tablespoon lemon juice
1	tablespoon boiling water
2	tablespoons butter, melted
$^1/_2$	teaspoon vanilla

In a small mixing bowl, combine sugar, lemon juice, butter, and vanilla. Gradually add water and mix until smooth. Spread over cooled Datenut Bars. Yield: 12 bars.

Deluxe Chocolate Bars

$1/3$	cup butter, soft
1	cup brown sugar plus $1/2$ cup
1	cup flour plus 2 tablespoons
2	eggs, beaten well
1	teaspoon vanilla
$1/2$	teaspoon salt
1	(6-ounce) package chocolate chips
1	cup pecans, chopped
	chocolate glaze

Preheat oven to 350 degrees. In a medium mixing bowl, cream butter, and $1/2$ cup brown sugar. Stir in 1 cup flour. Press in an ungreased 9 x 13-inch baking pan for 10 minutes. In another mixing bowl, combine eggs, remaining brown sugar, and vanilla. Stir in remaining flour, baking powder, and slat. Add chocolate chips and pecans. Spread over baked layer. Bake for 15–20 minutes. Cool.

Chocolate Glaze

1	tablespoon cocoa plus $1^1/2$ teaspoons
1	tablespoon butter plus 1 teaspoon
2	tablespoons boiling water
1	cup powdered sugar

In a medium saucepan, combine cocoa, butter, and water. Cook on low heat until thick and smooth. Beat in 1 cup powdered sugar until smooth. Yield: 12 bars.

Extra Chocolate Brownies

1/2	cup dark corn syrup
1/2	cup butter
5	(1-ounce) squares semi-sweet chocolate
3/4	cup sugar
3	eggs
1	teaspoon vanilla
1	cup flour, unsifted
1	cup pecans, chopped
	brownie icing

Preheat oven to 350 degrees. Grease and flour a 9-inch square cake pan. In a large saucepan, melt butter and add corn syrup. Bring this mixture to a boil. Remove from heat and add chocolate. Stir until melted. Add sugar, and stir in eggs, one at a time. Add vanilla, flour and pecans. Pour into pan and bake for 30 minutes. Cool. Glaze with brownie icing.

Brownie Icing

3	(1-ounce) semi-sweet chocolate squares
1	tablespoon butter
1	teaspoon milk
2	tablespoons corn syrup

In a small saucepan, melt chocolate with butter. Stir often. Remove from heat and stir in syrup and milk. Mix well and glaze brownies.

Donnie's Cherry Pie

Cherry pie has always been my favorite dessert. Have plenty of ice cream around and enjoy this delicious finale to your meal.

1	(16-ounce) can cherries, water packed
1½	cups sugar plus ½ cup
1	tablespoon sifted corn starch
1	tablespoon sifted flour
½	teaspoon salt
2	tablespoons butter plus 1 tablespoon
1	teaspoon almond extract
½	teaspoon lemon juice
½	teaspoon lemon zest
4	drops red food coloring
	Donnie's Pie Crust

Preheat oven to 400 degrees. Place cookie sheet in oven. In a medium saucepan, combine the liquid from the cherries, sugar, corn starch, flour, and salt. Cook until mixture is thick and bubbling. Add cherries and cook 5 more minutes. Add butter, almond extract, lemon juice, lemon zest, and food coloring. Put in unbaked pie crust and add top crust and dot with remaining butter and sugar. Bake on preheated cookie sheet for 10 minutes. Reduce heat to 350 degrees for 30 minutes or until mixture is set.

Donnie's Pie Crust

2	cups flour
1	cup shortening (I use Crisco)
¹/₂	teaspoon salt
5	tablespoons ice cold water

The key to the best crust is not to handle the dough very much. In a mixing bowl, incorporate flour, salt, and shortening with a pastry blender. Add the ice water all at once, and with your hands, work the water into the flour mixture. Quickly, you will be able to knead the dough into a ball. Add additional flour when completed and refrigerate at least 30 minutes. Roll out between 2 pieces of waxed paper and carefully remove top paper. Invert onto pie plate and remove other piece of waxed paper. You will have plenty of dough left for a top crust or cut in strips for a criss-cross pattern.

Texas Chocolate Cookies

¹/₂	cup butter, softened
¹/₂	cup granulated sugar
1	large egg
¹/₂	teaspoon vanilla extract
1¹/₂	cups all-purpose flour
¹/₂	teaspoon baking soda
1	cup confectioners' sugar
¹/₂	teaspoon salt
³/₄	cup semi-sweet chocolate chips
¹/₂	cup white chocolate chips
¹/₂	cup pecans, chopped
¹/₂	tablespoon water
¹/₂	tablespoon milk

Preheat oven to 350 degrees. In a large mixing bowl, beat butter, sugar, egg, and vanilla. Add slowly the flour, baking soda, and salt and beat until smooth. Put ¹/₂ cup semi-sweet chocolate, and white chocolate with pecans, in batter. Divide dough into 8 equal portions. Drop each on an ungreased cookie sheet. Press down. Bake cookies 12–15 minutes until golden brown. Cool completely.

Glaze
In a small saucepan, place ¹/₄ cup semi-sweet chocolate chips and melt. Remove from heat. In another small bowl, combine confectioners' sugar, ¹/₂ tablespoon water, and ¹/₂ tablespoon milk. Beat until smooth. Using separate spoons, drizzle chocolate and confectioners' icing over cooled cookies. Let stand about 10 minutes to set. Yield: 8 cookies.

Apple Pie

2	pounds tart apples, peeled and sliced
1	tablespoon lemon juice
³/₄	cup sugar
1	teaspoon cinnamon
2	tablespoons flour
¹/₈	teaspoon salt
²/₃	cup sifted flour
¹/₃	cup light brown sugar
¹/₃	cup butter
9	inch pie shell (See Donnie's Pie Crust) unbaked

In a medium-size bowl, toss together apples, lemon juice, sugar, cinnamon, and 2 tablespoons flour, and salt until coated. Place in the 9-inch pie shell. In another bowl, combine ²/₃ cup flour, brown sugar, and butter. Mix well. Sprinkle on top of apples and bake at 400 degrees for 40–45 minutes. Yield: 8 servings.

Homemade Ice Cream

On the hottest summer days, Mother made her wonderful vanilla ice cream. She'd prepare the eggs, milk, and cream mixture with fresh vanilla, while we would assemble the old crank-type freezer. An old weathered wooden bucket, a box of rock salt, and ice were all we needed. When we were tired of cranking, we would turn the job over to the next person. This freezer made better ice cream than you could buy, not to mention the fun we had in making it.

Our Favorite Chocolate Cake

2	eggs
2	cups sugar
$^1/_2$	cup cocoa
1	cup buttermilk
$2^1/_2$	cups flour
2	teaspoons soda
$^1/_2$	teaspoon salt
$1^1/_4$	cups oil
$^1/_8$	teaspoon cream of tartar
1	cup very hot water
	Chocolate Cake Icing

In a large mixing bowl, combine eggs, sugar, cocoa, buttermilk, flour, soda, salt, oil, and cream of tartar. Beat at high speed. Add hot water and beat 1 minute longer. Bake at 300 degrees for 30–40 minutes in 3 (8-inch) round cake pans. Cool completely on a wire rack and ice with Chocolate Cake Icing.

Chocolate Cake Icing

1	stick butter
6	tablespoons cocoa
1	(16-ounce) box powdered sugar
2	teaspoons vanilla
2	tablespoons milk

In the microwave, melt butter and add cocoa. Stir well and add to sugar. Add vanilla and milk. With a spatula or spoon, stir well until smooth.

The Best Brownies in Texas

³/₄	cup butter, melted
1¹/₂	cups sugar
1¹/₂	teaspoons vanilla
4	eggs
³/₄	cup unsifted all-purpose flour
¹/₂	cup cocoa
¹/₂	teaspoon baking powder
¹/₂	teaspoon salt
¹/₂	cup pecans, chopped

In a medium mixing bowl, combine butter, sugar, and vanilla. Add eggs and beat well. Combine in another bowl the flour, cocoa, baking powder, and salt. Gradually add to the egg mixture until well-blended. Spread in a greased 8-inch square pan. Bake at 350 degrees for 40–45 minutes or until brownie begins to pull away form the edges. Cool. Ice with Chocolate Cake Icing.

French Coconut Pie

1¹/₂	cups sugar
2	tablespoons flour
¹/₄	teaspoon salt
¹/₄	cup plus 2 tablespoons butter, melted
3	eggs, beaten
1	teaspoon vinegar
1	teaspoon vanilla
¹/₂–1	teaspoon coconut extract
¹/₄	teaspoon almond extract
1	(3¹/₂-ounce) can flaked coconut
1	unbaked 9-inch pastry shell (see Donnie's Pie Crust)

Preheat oven to 350 degrees. Combine sugar, flour, and salt in a medium bowl. Add butter, mixing well. Add eggs and beat until blended. Add vinegar, vanilla, and coconut. Pour filling into pastry shell. Bake for 45 minutes or until set. Shield with foil after 25 minutes. Yield: 6 pieces.

French Silk Pie

2	squares unsweetened chocolate (6 tablespoons cocoa, 2 tablespoons butter)
1	teaspoon vanilla
³/₄	cup butter
1	cup sugar
3	eggs

Melt and cool chocolate. Cream butter and sugar. Add chocolate and vanilla and mix together. Add one egg at a time and beat 4 minutes per egg at medium speed. Pour into pie shell. Top with whipped cream. Sprinkle with chocolate crumbs. Refrigerate several hours.

Heaven's Cake

2¹/₂	cups sugar
1	cup shortening
2	eggs, well beaten
2	tablespoons cocoa
¹/₄	teaspoon salt
2	teaspoons soda
2	cups buttermilk
3	cups flour, sifted
1	teaspoon vanilla

Preheat oven to 350 degrees. Grease and flour 3 (9-inch) round cake pans. In a medium mixing bowl, cream sugar and shortening. Add eggs, cocoa, salt, soda, buttermilk, flour, and vanilla. After well incorporated, divide equally in the prepared cake pans. Bake for 25–30 minutes or until done.

Heaven's Cake Icing

¹/₂	stick margarine
2	eggs, beaten
2	cups sugar
1	cup evaporated milk
1	can coconut
¹/₂	cup pecans, chopped

In a medium saucepan, combine margarine, eggs, sugar, and milk. Cook until thick, stirring constantly. Remove from heat and add coconut and pecans. Ice cooled cake. Yield: 10 servings.

German Chocolate Cake

2	(1-ounce) squares sweetened chocolate
2¹/₂	cups all-purpose flour
1¹/₂	teaspoons baking soda
¹/₄	teaspoon salt
1	cup butter, softened
1¹/₂	cups sugar
4	extra-large eggs, separated
2	teaspoons vanilla
1¹/₄	cups buttermilk
	German Chocolate Cake Frosting

Preheat oven to 350 degrees. Grease and flour 3 (9-inch) round cake pans. Melt chocolate in a double boiler and set aside to cool. Sift together the flour, baking soda, and salt. In a separate bowl, cream the butter and sugar. Add the egg yolks one at a time beating well after each addition. Beat in vanilla. Stir in the cooled chocolate and mix until blended. Add the dry ingredients alternately with buttermilk to chocolate mixture, ending with the dry ingredients. In another bowl, beat the egg whites until they hold soft peaks. Fold egg whites into batter and mix well. Divide batter among the prepared pans. Bake for 25 minutes. Cool for 10 minutes in the pans, and place onto wire racks to cool completely. Spread frosting on tops of layers and stack. Yield: 10 servings.

German Chocolate Cake Frosting

¹/₂	cup butter, cubed
1	cup evaporated milk
¹/₂	cup dark brown sugar, firmly packed
3	extra-large egg yolks, lightly beaten
1	teaspoon vanilla
1	cup flaked, sweetened coconut
1	cup pecans, chopped

In a small saucepan, combine butter, milk, and sugar. Cook over low heat. In a small cup, place the egg yolks and add ¹/₄ cup milk mixture and stir until well-blended. Slowly add the yolk mixture to the heated mixture and slowly heat stirring constantly for 12–15 minutes. Stir in vanilla. When the mixture has cooled, stir in coconut and pecans. Cool completely before icing cake.

Hummingbird Cake

3	cups all-purpose flour
2	cups sugar
1	teaspoon baking soda
1	teaspoon salt
1	teaspoon cinnamon
3	eggs, beaten
1	cup vegetable oil
1½	teaspoon vanilla extract
1	(8-ounce) can crushed pineapple, undrained
1	cup pecans, chopped
2	cups bananas, chopped
	Cream Cheese Frosting

Preheat oven to 350 degrees. Grease and flour 3 (9-inch) round cake pans. In a medium mixing bowl, combine flour, sugar, baking soda, salt, and cinnamon. Add eggs and oil. Stir in vanilla, pineapple, pecans, and bananas. Mix well. Divide batter into the prepared cake pans. Bake for 25–30 minutes. Cool in pans for 10 minutes and place onto wire rack to finish cooling. Spread frosting between layers and on top and sides of cake.

Cream Cheese Frosting

1	(8-ounce) package cream cheese, softened
½	cup butter, softened
1	(16-ounce) box powdered sugar
1	teaspoon vanilla
½	cup pecans, chopped

In a medium mixing bowl, combine cream cheese and butter, beating until smooth. Add powdered sugar and vanilla. Beat until light and fluffy. Ice cake and garnish with pecans. Yield: 12 servings.

Italian Cream Cake

1	stick margarine
½	cup shortening
2	cups sugar
5	eggs, separated
2	cups all-purpose flour
1	teaspoon soda
1	cup buttermilk
1	teaspoon vanilla
1	(3⅓–ounce) can flaked coconut
1	cup pecans, chopped
	Cream Cheese Frosting

Preheat oven to 350 degrees. Grease and flour 3 (9-inch) round cake pans. In a medium mixing bowl, cream margarine and shortening. Add sugar and beat until mixture is smooth. Add egg yolks and beat well. In another bowl, sift flour and soda. Add flour mixture alternating with buttermilk to the cream mixture. Stir in vanilla. Add coconut and pecans. In another mixing bowl, beat until stiff the egg whites. Combine whites with batter and pour into the prepared cake pans. Bake 25 minutes or until cake tests done. Cool on wire racks and frost between layers and top and sides with Cream Cheese Frosting. Yield: 12 servings.

Mother's Jelly Roll

Of all the people in the world, my mother, Geraldine McLauchlin Lewis, was the most wonderful cook I've ever known. We lived in the country, several milks from the nearest grocery store, and with seven children and a husband to cook for each day, she had to be creative. This Jelly Roll recipe was an afters-chool snack we kids often enjoyed.

3	eggs
1	cup granulated sugar
1/3	cup watered sugar
1	teaspoon vanilla
3/4	cup flour
1	teaspoon baking powder
1/4	teaspoon salt
2/3	cup grape jelly
1	(16-ounce) box powdered sugar

Preheat oven to 375 degrees. Line jelly roll pan (15 x 10-inch) with waxed paper and grease generously. In a small mixing bowl, beat eggs on high speed until very thick and lemon colored, about 5 minutes. Pour eggs into a larger mixing bowl, and add sugar, beating well. Beat in water and vanilla on low speed. Add flour, baking powder, and salt gradually, beating just until batter is smooth. Pour into pan. Bake about 12–15 minutes or until cake tests done. Invert onto towel sprinkled with powdered sugar. Carefully remove paper. While still hot, carefully roll cake and towel from narrow end. Cool on wire rack at least 30 minutes. Unroll cake and remove towel. Beat jelly slightly with fork to soften. Spread over cake. Roll up and sprinkle with powdered sugar. Yield: 10 servings.

Ladybars

3	eggs
¹/₂	cup granulated sugar
¹/₂	cup sifted cake flour
¹/₂	teaspoon vanilla
3	tablespoons confectioners' sugar
1	tablespoon granulated sugar

Preheat oven to 350 degrees. Grease and flour a baking sheet. In a small mixing bowl, beat egg yolks, and ¹/₂ cup granulated sugar. Gently fold in cake flour and vanilla. Beat until smooth. Batter will be thick. Beat egg whites in another bowl until stiff peaks form. Gently fold in the yolk-sugar mixture until combined. Drop 2 teaspoons batter, side by side, on cookie sheet. Shape into oval finger about 3 inches long and 1 inch wide. Combine powdered sugar and 1 tablespoon granulated sugar and sprinkle over bars. Let stand 5 minutes before baking. Bake for 8 minutes. Cool on wire racks. Yield: 5 dozen.

Lemon Date Squares

¹/₂	cup butter, softened
1	cup flour, plus 2 tablespoons, sifted
1	teaspoon grated lemon rind
2	eggs
1	cup sugar
¹/₂	teaspoon baking powder
¹/₂	teaspoon salt
¹/₂	cup chopped dates
1	(3¹/₂-ounce) can sweetened flaked coconut
1	teaspoon lemon juice
¹/₄	cup powdered sugar

Preheat oven to 350 degrees. Butter bottom of a square 8 x 8 x 2-inch baking pan. In a medium mixing bowl, cream butter until light and fluffy. Blend in 1 cup flour and lemon rind. Pat into bottom of prepared pan. Bake for 20 minutes. Removed from oven. Beat eggs in medium bowl until foamy. Add sugar gradually and beat until thick and lemon-colored. Blend in 2 tablespoons flour, baking powder, salt, dates, coconut, and lemon juice. Spoon over baked crust. Bake 25 minutes longer. Cool and cut into squares. Sprinkle with powdered sugar. Yield: 12 squares.

Lemon Bars

These are our most popular bar cookies. They are sweet, lemony, and delightful just out of the oven. They're a great addition to your dessert party tray when cut in 1-inch squares and placed in pastry cups.

2	cups flour
1/2	cup sugar
1	cup butter
4	large eggs, slightly beaten
5	tablespoons flour
2	cups sugar
1/4	cup lemon juice
1	lemon rind, grated
1/2	cup confectioners' sugar

Preheat oven to 350 degrees. Line a 9 x 13-inch baking pan with waxed paper. Combine 2 cups flour and 1/2 cup sugar in mixing bowl. Add butter. Work the mixture with your hands until well-blended. Press into prepared pan and bake for 15 minutes. In another mixing bowl, combine eggs and 2 cups sugar. Add 5 tablespoons flour gradually. Mix in lemon juice and rind. Spread mixture over baked crust and bake 15–20 minutes longer until crust is light brown. Cool in the pan. Cut into 2-inch squares and dust with confectioners' sugar. Yield: 16 squares.

Macaroons

2²/₃	cups sweetened coconut, flaked
²/₃	cup sugar
¹/₄	cup flour
¹/₄	teaspoon salt
4	egg whites
1	teaspoon almond extract
1	cup pecans, chopped

Preheat oven to 325 degrees. Grease lightly your thickest cookie sheet. In a medium mixing bowl, combine sugar, coconut, flour, and salt. Stir in egg whites and extract. Stir in pecans. Drop in tablespoon-size balls onto prepared cookie sheet, and bake for 20–25 minutes or until golden brown. Yield: 24 cookies.

Lemon Tarts

2	cups flour plus 4 tablespoons
1½	sticks margarine
2	egg yolks
1	(4½-ounce) box lemon pudding and pie filling
¾	cup sugar
3	egg yolks
½	cup lemon juice
2¼	cups water
2	cups whipped non-dairy topping

Preheat oven to 300 degrees. In a small mixing bowl, combine 2 cups flour and sugar. Add butter and crumble it onto the flour with your hands or pastry blender. Stir in 2 egg yolks until well-blended. Work dough with your hands until smooth. Press a small amount of pastry in each miniature muffin pan. Bake for 30 minutes or until pastry is browned. Allow to cool. Fill with lemon filling. In a small saucepan, combine pudding mix, sugar, lemon juice, and 3 egg yolks. Slowly add water. Cook and stir over medium heat until mixture comes to a boil. Allow to cool completely and fill tart shells. Place a dab of whipped topping on top for garnish followed by grated lemon rind if desired.

Coconut Bars

¹/₂	cup butter
1¹/₂	cups graham cracker crumbs
1	(14-ounce) can sweetened condensed milk
1	(3¹/₂-ounce) can coconut
1	cup pecans, chopped
1	(6-ounce) package chocolate chips

Preheat oven to 350 degrees. In a small mixing bowl, combine butter and cracker crumbs. Press in the bottom of an 8 x 8-inch pan. In another mixing bowl, combine milk, coconut, pecans, and chocolate chips. Pour milk mixture over the crust and bake for 25–30 minutes. Yield: 12 bars.

Mother's Cookies

1	cup sugar
1	cup brown sugar
1	cup shortening
2	eggs
2	teaspoon vanilla
2	cups flour
1	teaspoon baking powder
1	teaspoon soda
1	teaspoon salt
1⅓	cups coconut
1	cup pecans, chopped
2	cups oatmeal

Preheat oven to 375 degrees. In a medium mixing bowl, cream sugars and shortening. Add eggs and vanilla. Mix well. In another bowl, sift flour, baking powder, soda, and salt. Stir into creamed mixture. Mix in coconut, oatmeal, and pecans. Bake for 12 minutes. Cool on wire rack. Yield: 2 dozen cookies.

Marble Fudge Bars

1	cup margarine
2¹/₂	cups sugar
1	cup all-purpose flour
1	cup walnuts, chopped
1	(8-ounce) package cream cheese, softened
4	(1-ounce) squares unsweetened chocolate
4	eggs
¹/₂	teaspoon salt
2	teaspoons vanilla

Preheat oven to 350 degrees. Grease a 9 x 13-inch baking pan. In a large heavy saucepan, melt butter and chocolate. With wire whisk or spoon, beat in 2 cups sugar and 3 eggs until well-blended. Stir in flour, salt, nuts, and 1 teaspoon vanilla. Pour and spread evenly in prepared pan. In small bowl, beat cream cheese, ¹/₂ cup sugar, 1 egg, and 1 teaspoon vanilla until well-blended. With a large spoon, drop the cheese mixture in spoonfuls on top of batter in pan. "Using a knife, lightly make a criss-cross pattern in the batter. Bake for 40–45 minutes until cake tests done. Cool on rack and cut into bars. Refrigerate. Yield: 16 bars.

Mini-Cheesecakes

12	vanilla wafers
2	(8-ounce) packages cream cheese, softened
½	cup sugar
1	teaspoon vanilla
2	eggs

Preheat oven to 325 degrees. Line muffin tins with foil liners. Place 1 vanilla wafer in each liner. In a medium mixing bowl, combine cream cheese, vanilla, and sugar until well-blended. Add eggs. Mix well. Pour over wafers, filling ¾ full. Bake for 25 minutes. Remove from pan when cool. Chill. Top with fruit, preserves, nuts, or chocolate. Yield: 12 servings.

Mississippi Mud Bars

1½	cups flour
2	cups sugar
2	tablespoons cocoa
4	eggs
2	sticks butter, plus ½ cup, softened
1	tablespoon vanilla plus 1 teaspoon
1	(3½-ounce) can coconut, flaked
1½	cups pecans, plus 1 cup, chopped
1	jar marshmallow crème
6	tablespoons cocoa
2	tablespoons oil
1	(16-ounce) box confectioners' sugar

Preheat oven to 325 degrees. Grease and flour a jelly roll pan. In a medium mixing bowl, combine flour, sugar, and 2 tablespoons cocoa. Add eggs and 2 sticks butter. Mix well. Stir in vanilla, coconut, and nuts. Bake for 30–35 minutes. While hot, spread the marshmallow crème evenly. Let cool. In another saucepan, melt ½ cup butter, 6 tablespoons cocoa, and oil. Add to confectioners' sugar, 1 teaspoon vanilla and 1 cup pecans. Pour and spread evenly the chocolate/nut mixture over marshmallow cream layer. Cut into bars. Yield: 16 bars.

Oatmeal Cookies

2	cups flour
1	teaspoon baking powder
¹/₂	teaspoon salt
1	teaspoon soda
1	cup shortening
1	cup sugar
1	cup brown sugar
¹/₂	teaspoon vanilla
2	eggs
¹/₂	cup pecans, chopped
1¹/₂	cups oatmeal

Preheat oven to 375 degrees. In a medium mixing bowl, cream sugars, shortening, and vanilla. Add eggs. Add flour, baking powder, salt, and soda. Fold in pecans and oatmeal. Mix well. Use a tablespoon of batter, and drop onto ungreased cookie sheet and bake for 10–15 minutes. Yield: 2 dozen.

Old Fashioned Brownies

4	eggs
2	cups sugar
²/₃	cups shortening, melted
2	(1-ounce) squares semi-sweet chocolate
1	teaspoon salt
2	teaspoons vanilla
³/₄	cup cocoa
5	tablespoons oil
1¹/₂	cups flour
2	cups pecans, chopped

Preheat oven to 325 degrees. Grease and flour a 9 x 13-inch baking pan. In a medium mixing bowl, combine eggs and sugar. Add salt and vanilla. Set aside. In a small saucepan, melt shortening, oil, chocolate, and cocoa. Add to sugar mixture. Stir in flour and nuts. Bake for 30 minutes. Icing is optional.

Orange Bars

1	cup sour cream
1	teaspoon soda
1	cup shortening
1	cup sugar
2	eggs
½	cup orange juice
4½	cups flour
2	teaspoons salt
1	teaspoon vanilla

Preheat oven to 400 degrees. Grease and flour a 9 x 13-inch baking pan. In a small bowl, combine sour cream and soda. In another bowl, cream shortening and sugar. Add eggs and orange juice. Add flour, baking powder, and salt alternately with sour cream mixture. Add vanilla. Bake for 12 minutes in prepared pan. Frost with the following icing.

Orange Bars Icing

1½	cups powdered sugar
3	tablespoons butter, melted
2	tablespoons orange juice
1	tablespoon orange rind, grated

In medium mixing bowl, combine butter and orange juice. Add orange rind and mix in powdered sugar. Stir well. Ice bars while warm. Yield: 15 bars.

Peanut Butter Bars

¹/₂	cup shortening
¹/₂	cup brown sugar
¹/₂	cup granulated sugar
³/₄	cup peanut butter
2	eggs
2	tablespoons milk
1¹/₂	cups flour
¹/₂	teaspoon salt
¹/₂	teaspoon soda

Preheat oven to 350 degrees. Grease and flour a 9 x 13-inch baking pan. In a large mixing bowl, combine shortening, brown sugar, granulated sugar, and peanut butter. Add eggs and milk. Beat well. Stir in flour, salt, and soda. Bake in prepared pan for 20 minutes. Sift powdered sugar over bars for garnish. Yield: 12 bars.

Peanut Dandies

½	cup sugar, plus 2 tablespoons
½	cup brown sugar
½	cup shortening
½	cup peanut butter
1	egg
2	tablespoons milk
1¾	cups flour
2	teaspoons soda
½	teaspoon salt
1	teaspoon vanilla
1	(9-ounce) package chocolate kisses

Preheat oven to 375 degrees. In a medium mixing bowl, combine sugars, shortening, and peanut butter. Add the egg and milk. Stir in flour, soda, and salt. Add vanilla. Roll into a ball. Roll balls in remaining sugar. Bake for 10–12 minutes on an ungreased cookie sheet. Place the chocolate kisses in center of each. Cool. Yield: 48 dandies.

Lewis's Pecan Pie

4	eggs
1	cup sugar
¹/₂	teaspoon salt
¹/₃	cup margarine, melted
1	cup corn syrup
1	cup pecan halves
1	(9-inch) unbaked pastry shell

Preheat oven to 375 degrees. In a medium mixing bowl, beat eggs, sugar, salt, margarine, and syrup. Stir in pecans. Pour into pastry lined pie plate. Bake for 40–50 minutes. Cool slightly. Yield: 8 pieces.

Pumpkin Cheesecake Bars

1	cup all-purpose flour
1/3	cup brown sugar, firmly packed
5	tablespoons butter, softened
1/2	cup pecans, chopped finely
1	(8-ounce) package cream cheese, softened
3/4	cup sugar
1/2	cup solid packed pumpkin
2	eggs, beaten
1 1/2	teaspoons cinnamon
1	teaspoon allspice
1	teaspoon vanilla

Preheat oven to 350 degrees. In a medium mixing bowl, combine flour and brown sugar. Cut in butter using a pastry blender. Stir in nuts. Set aside 3/4 cup mixture for topping. Press remaining mixture into bottom of 8 x 8-inch baking pan. Bake in oven for 15 minutes. Cool slightly. Combine cream cheese, sugar, pumpkin, eggs, cinnamon, allspice, and vanilla in a large mixing bowl. Blend until smooth. Pour over baked crust. Sprinkle reserved topping when completed. Bake for 30–35 minutes. Cool before cutting into bars. Yield: 24 bars.

Warm Bittersweet Chocolate Cupcakes

¹/₂	cup plus 6 tablespoons whipping cream
2	tablespoons (¹/₄ stick) unsalted butter
1	tablespoon unsweetened cocoa
8	ounces bittersweet chocolate
2	large eggs
¹/₄	cup sugar
¹/₂	cup ground pecan
1	teaspoon vanilla
	vanilla ice cream

Preheat oven to 350. Butter 9¹/₃ inch muffin cups. Sprinkle with sugar, shake out excess. Bring ¹/₂ cup cream, butter, and cocoa to boil in heavy saucepan, whisking until smooth. Remove from heat. Add 5 ounces chocolate. Stir until melted. Cool 10 minutes. Beat eggs with ¹/₄ cup sugar in medium bowl about 8 minutes. Gently fold in pecans and vanilla. Fold in chocolate mixture. Divide batter among muffin cups. Bake cupcakes until puffed and knife inserted into center comes out clean, about 18 minutes. Cool in pan on rack 10 minutes. Cake centers will sink. Turn out cakes. Arrange warm cakes upside down on plates. Spoon chocolate glaze over. Serve with ice cream.

Chocolate Marble Brownies

¹/₂	cup butter
4	(1-ounce) squares semi-sweet chocolate
1	(1-ounce) square unsweetened chocolate
3	eggs
³/₄	cup granulated sugar
¹/₂	cup all-purpose flour
¹/₄	teaspoon baking soda
1	(8-ounce) package cream cheese, softened
¹/₄	teaspoon almond extract

Preheat oven to 350 degrees. Grease and flour an 8 x 8-inch square baking pan. In a heavy saucepan, melt butter and chocolates. Stir untl smooth. Remove from heat. In another bowl, beat 2 eggs, ¹/₂ cup sugar, flour, and baking soda. Add to the chocolate mixture. In another mixing bowl, beat cream cheese, remaining egg, ¹/₄ cup sugar, and almond extract until blended and smooth. Spoon the chocolate and creamed mixtures alternately into prepared pan. Run spatula through batter to produce a marbled effect. Bake 30 minutes. Cool in pan for 10 minutes. Remove from pan and top with our Chocolate Cake Icing. Yield: 6 servings.

Red Velvet Cake

2½	cups shortening
1½	cups sugar
2	eggs
1	teaspoon butter flavoring
1	teaspoon vanilla
2	tablespoons cocoa
2	drops red food coloring
2½	cups cake flour
1	teaspoon salt
1	teaspoon soda
1	cup buttermilk
1	tablespoon vinegar

Preheat oven to 350 degrees. Grease and flour 3 (8-inch) round cake pans. In a large mixing bowl, cream shortening and add sugar gradually until light and fluffy. Add eggs one at a time, beating after each addition. Add butter and vanilla flavorings. Make a paste of cocoa and food coloring and blend in. Sift flour, salt, and soda. Add to cream mixture and alternate with buttermilk. Add vinegar with last part of buttermilk and beat until smooth. Bake for 20–25 minutes or until cake tests done. Cool in pans for 10 minutes. Remove from pan and cool completely. Ice between layers and top and sides with the following frosting

Red Velvet Cake Frosting

1	(16-ounce) box powdered sugar
1	tablespoon vanilla
½	cup shortening
½	teaspoon salt
¼	teaspoon butter flavoring
5	tablespoons milk

In a large mixing bowl, sift sugar and salt. Add vanilla, shortening, and butter flavoring. Mix well. Add milk to make mixture creamy. Yield: 12 slices.

Sand Tarts

1	cup butter
4	tablespoons powdered sugar
2	cups flour
1½	teaspoons baking powder
½	teaspoon salt
1	tablespoon vanilla
1	cup pecans, finely chopped

Preheat oven to 375 degrees. In a medium mixing bowl, cream butter and sugar. Sift flour, baking powder, and salt and add to creamed butter. Add vanilla and nuts. Drop by teaspoon one inch apart on a greased cookie sheet. Bake for 10 minutes or until brown. Dust with powdered sugar if desired. Yield: 4 dozen cookies.

Sour Cream Banana Bars

1¹/₂	cups sugar
1	cup sour cream
¹/₂	cup margarine
2	eggs
1¹/₂	cup bananas, mashed
2	teaspoons vanilla
1	teaspoon salt
1	teaspoon soda
2	cups flour
¹/₂	cup pecans, chopped
	Banana Bar Frosting

Preheat oven to 375 degrees. Grease and flour a 9 x 13-inch baking pan. In a large mixing bowl, cream sugar, sour cream, margarine, and eggs. Beat for 1 minute. Beat in bananas and vanilla. Sift in flour, salt, and soda. Stir in pecans. Bake for 20–25 minutes. Frost when cooled.

Banana Bar Frosting

¹/₂	cup margarine
2	cups powdered sugar
1	teaspoon vanilla
3	tablespoons milk
1	teaspoon banana flavoring

In medium mixing bowl, combine butter and orange juice. Add orange rind and mix in powdered sugar. Stir well. Ice bars while warm. Yield: 15 bars.

Strawberry Banana Pie

1	(3-ounce) box strawberry Jell-O
1	cup sugar
4	tablespoons cornstarch
1	tablespoon lemon juice
15	drops red food coloring
3	bananas, sliced
2	pints strawberries, sliced
1	cooked pie crust (See Donnie's Pie Crust)
1	(½ pint) carton whipping cream
3	tablespoons sugar
½	teaspoon vanilla

In a medium saucepan, bring to a boil Jell-O according to directions on package. Add sugar, cornstarch, lemon juice, and food coloring. Cool until slightly set. Slice bananas and place strawberries in cooked pie shell. Sprinkle with powdered sugar. Pour cooled Jell-O mixture over all. Let this be refrigerated until set. In a small mixing bowl, beat whipped cream until is forms stiff peaks and add sugar and vanilla. Yield: 8 slices.

Velvet Almond Fudge Cake

1½	cups almonds, slivered
1	(12-ounce) package chocolate chips
1	package chocolate or fudge cake mix
1	(4-ounce) package instant chocolate pudding mix
4	eggs
1	cup sour cream
½	cup water
¼	cup oil
½	teaspoon vanilla
½	teaspoon almond extract
	whipped cream

Preheat oven to 350 degrees. Grease and flour a 9 x 13-inch baking pan. In another pan, place slivered almonds in oven to toast for 3 to 5 minutes. Place ½ cup of the almonds on the bottom of the prepared pan. In a mixing bowl, place fudge cake mix, pudding mix, eggs, sour cream, water, oil, vanilla, and almond extracts. Blend at medium speed for 4 minutes. Stir in chocolate chips and remaining almonds. Pour into prepared pan. Bake for 70 minutes or until cake begins to pull away from the sides of the pan. Cool in pan for 15 minutes. Garnish with whipped cream. Yield: 15 pieces.

Toffee Bars

4¹/₂	cups oatmeal, uncooked
1	cup brown sugar, firmly packed
³/₄	cup margarine, melted
¹/₂	cup corn syrup
1	tablespoon vanilla
¹/₂	teaspoon salt
1	(12-ounce) package semi-sweet chocolate chips
2	tablespoons shortening
²/₃	cup pecans, chopped

Preheat oven to 450 degrees. Grease and flour a 10 x 15-inch baking pan. In a large mixing bowl, combine oatmeal, sugar, margarine, syrup, vanilla, and salt. Mix well. Firmly press mixture in bottom of pan. Bake 12 minutes until brown. Cool completely. In a saucepan over low heat, melt chocolate and shortening, stirring until smooth. Spread evenly over the oat base. Sprinkle with pecans. Chill until set. Cut into bars. Yield: 60 bars.

Vanilla Bars

2	cups flour
1/2	cup sugar
1	cup butter
1	(8-ounce) package cream cheese
2	eggs
2	teaspoons vanilla
1	(16-ounce) box powdered sugar

Preheat oven to 350 degrees. In a small mixing bowl, combine flour and sugar. Put in butter with pastry blender. Press into a 9 x 13-inch pan. Bake 15 minutes until golden brown. In another mixing bowl, combine cream cheese, eggs, vanilla, and powdered sugar. Beat 3 minutes and pour over prepared crust. Bake for 40 minutes. Yield: 12 bars.

Pear Cake

2	cups sugar
4	cups pears, peeled and sliced
1	cup pecans
2	eggs
1	cup oil
1	teaspoon vanilla
3	cups flour
1/2	teaspoon salt
3/4	teaspoon cinnamon
3/4	teaspoon nutmeg
2	teaspoons soda

Preheat oven to 350 degrees. Grease and flour a bunt pan. In a medium mixing bowl, combine sugar, pecans, and pears. Let sit for 2 minutes. Add eggs, oil, and vanilla. Sift in flour, salt, cinnamon, nutmeg, and soda. Stir well to blend. Pour into prepared pan and bake for 1 hour and 15 minutes. Yield: 12 slices.

Our Two Pear Trees

Near the house grow two large pear trees. I am not sure how old they are, but I know they produce the largest pears I have ever seen. The pears are canned or eaten fresh. The trees continue to bear fruit, which is enjoyed at many homes of family and friends.

Hot Fudge Sauce

1	cup powdered sugar
1/2	cup (1 stick) unsalted butter, cut into pieces
1/2	cup whipping cream
4	ounces semisweet chocolate chopped
4	ounces unsweetened chocolate chopped
2	teaspoons vanilla extract

Combine powdered sugar, butter, and cream in heavy medium saucepan. Stir over medium-low heat until smooth. Remove from heat. Add chocolates and stir until melted and smooth. Stir in vanilla extract. Cover and chill. Re-warm over low heat before serving.

Bavarian Apple Torte

Crust

³/₄	cup butter, softened
¹/₂	cup granulated sugar
1¹/₂	cups all purpose flour
¹/₂	teaspoon vanilla extract

Filling

1	(8-ounce) package cream cheese, softened
¹/₄	cup granulated sugar
1	large egg
³/₄	teaspoon vanilla extract

Topping

3	cups thinly-sliced, peeled tart apples
¹/₂	cup granulated sugar
1	teaspoon ground cinnamon

Combine ingredients for crust in food processor and press onto the bottom of an ungreased 9 inch springform pan. In a mixing bowl, beat the cream cheese and sugar, add eggs and vanilla, mixing well. Pour over crust. Combine topping ingredients and spoon over filling. Place pan on a foil-lined baking sheet to prevent drips. Bake at 350 for 55–60 minutes or until the center is set and apples are tender. Cool completely on wire rack before releasing sides of pan. Store in the refrigerator. Yield: 12 servings.

Lewis's Berry Pound Cake

1	cup flour
$^1/_2$	teaspoon baking soda
$^1/_2$	teaspoon salt
3	cups sugar
1	cup butter
4	eggs
1	tablespoon vanilla
1	cup buttermilk
$^3/_4$	cup each: cranberries, orange juice, orange zest, cointreau, sugar
$^3/_4$	cup each blueberries, lemon juice, sugar, lemon zest

Mix batter and add $^2/_3$ to the cranberry mixture and $^1/_3$ to the blueberry. Place $^1/_3$ of the batter (cranberry) in prepared pan, then the blueberry mixture, then rest of the cranberry.

Glaze
1 cup powdered sugar, 4 teaspoons OJ, $^1/_2$ teaspoon orange peel, 1 tablespoon cointreau, toasted sliced almonds.

Blueberry–Lemon Cake with Lemon Cream Frosting

2	cups plus 6 tablespoons cake flour
2	teaspoons baking powder
1	teaspoon salt
3	cups fresh blueberries
1	cup whole milk
2	teaspoons vanilla extract
1	teaspoon grated lemon peel
1	cup butter (room temperature)
1½	cups sugar
4	large eggs
	lemon cream cheese frosting

Preheat oven to 350. Line bottom of pan with butter and flour. Sift flour, baking powder, salt. Use 1 tablespoon in another bowl and dust blueberries. Beat butter until creamy. Beat in eggs 1 at a time. Beat in flour mixture alternating with milk mixture. Fold in blueberries. Divide. Cook for 25 minutes.

Lemon Cream Cheese Frosting

16	ounces cream cheese
¾	cup butter
4	cups powdered sugar
1	teaspoon grated lemon peel
1	teaspoon vanilla

Cover and chill about 30 minutes, just firm enough to spread.

Buttermilk Cake

1	cup cake flour
3	teaspoons baking powder
$^1/_2$	teaspoon baking soda
$^1/_2$	teaspoon salt
3	sticks butter, room temp
2	cups sugar
4	large eggs
2	teaspoons vanilla
$1^1/_3$	cups buttermilk

Preheat oven to 350. Line pan or cupcake pans. Sift flour, baking powder, soda, and salt, set aside. Cream butter and sugar until fluffy, about 3 minutes. Add eggs one at a time. Stir in vanilla. Alternately add flour and buttermilk, ending with the flour. Bake.

Caramelized Walnuts

$^1/_2$	cup sugar
2	tablespoon balsamic vinegar
$1^1/_2$	cup walnuts

Toss to coat. Bake 10 minutes at 325.

Chewy Oatmeal Cookies

1¹/₂	cups all purpose flour
1	teaspoon baking soda
¹/₂	teaspoon salt
¹/₂	teaspoon cinnamon
2¹/₂	cups old fashioned oats
1	cup (8 ounce) unsalted butter (slightly soft, not warm)
1	cup packed light brown sugar
¹/₂	cup granulated sugar
2	large eggs
1	tablespoon honey
2	teaspoons vanilla

Optional:
Nuts
Cranberries

Set oven to 350. Lightly grease cookie sheet or line with parchment. Mix flour, baking soda, salt, and cinnamon in bowl. Stir in oats. Beat butter and both sugars until light and fluffy. Add eggs one at a time. Add honey and vanilla and beat until well blended. Add flour mixture in two additions.

Drop dough at least 2 inches apart using scoop. Bake until the centers of the cookies are soft and no longer wet. About 9 to 11 minutes. Let cool for 5 minutes. Cool completely on wire rack.

Coconut Macaroons

14	ounce package sweetened flaked coconut
14	ounce can sweetened condensed milk
1	teaspoon vanilla
2	large egg whites
¼	teaspoon salt

Preheat oven to 325. Line 2 baking sheets with parchment paper. Combine flaked coconut, milk, and vanilla extract in large bowl using electric mixer. Beat egg whites and salt in medium bowl until medium firm peaks. Fold ¹/₃ of the egg whites into coconut mixture to lighten then fold in remaining egg whites. Drop half of the coconut mixture by level tablespoonfulls onto baking sheets, spacing 2 inches apart. Top each with a second level tablespoonfull of coconut mixture. Bake until golden, about 25 minutes. Cool. Great with an iced coffee for a summer treat.

Chocolate Cake with Raspberry Filling

2	cups sugar
1³/₄	cups all purpose flour
³/₄	cup cocoa
1¹/₂	teaspoons baking powder
1¹/₂	teaspoons baking soda
1	teaspoon salt
2	eggs
1	cup milk
¹/₂	cup vegetable oil
2	teaspoons vanilla extract
1	cup boiling water

Heat oven to 350 degrees. Grease and flour 3 8-inch baking pans. Combine dry ingredients in large bowl. Add eggs, milk, oil, and vanilla. Beat for 2 minutes. Stir in boiling water. Pour into prepared pans. Bake 30 minutes or until wooden pick in center comes out clean. Cool 10 minutes. Remove from pans onto wire racks. Cool completely.

Raspberry Filling

2	cups mashed, fresh or frozen raspberries
3	tablespoons sugar
2	tablespoons cornstarch
2	tablespoons unsalted butter

In a saucepan, combine fruit, sugar, and cornstarch and whisk until smooth. Place over medium-low heat and cook, whisking constantly, until thickened, about 5 minutes. Remove from heat, add butter, and stir until smooth and let cool completely.

Chocolate Frosting

2	sticks butter (1 cup)
1¹/₃	cups cocoa
6	cups powdered sugar
²/₃	cup milk
2	teaspoons vanilla

Melt butter. Stir in cocoa. Alternate powdered sugar and milk, beating on medium speed. Stir in vanilla. Makes about 4 cups.

Coffee Brownies

2	cups sugar
15	tablespoons unsalted butter
³/₄	cup unsweetened cocoa powder
3	tablespoons instant coffee
¹/₂	teaspoon salt
3	large eggs
1¹/₄	teaspoons vanilla extract
1¹/₄	cups all purpose flour
³/₄	cup pecan pieces
1	cup semisweet chocolate chips
6	tablespoons freshly brewed coffee

Preheat oven to 350. Spray 13 x 9-2 inch metal pan with nonstick spray. Combine sugar, butter, cocoa, instant coffee, and salt in a large metal bowl. Place bowl over saucepan of simmering water and whisk until butter melts and ingredients are blended. Remove bowl from over water and cool to lukewarm if necessary. Whisk in eggs and vanilla. Sift flour over and fold in. Mix in pecans. Spread butter in prepared pan. Bake brownies until tester comes out clean, about 25 minutes. Cool brownies in pan. Place chocolate chips in small bowl. Bring brewed coffee to simmer in saucepan and pour over chips and stir until melted and smooth. Let cool and then carefully spread over brownies.

Pendulum Apple Pie

Pie Crust

1½	cups flour
½	cup butter
¼	cup ice-cold water

Place flour in a bowl. Cut in pieces of butter with a pastry blender until mixture resembles peas. Add water gradually, using a fork to gather the dough. Divide into two. When dough is ready for use, fold it in half and slide into a pie plate. Refrigerate for 30 minutes. Use the other dough for the top crust. Crimp edges with fork or finger to seal.

Pie Filling

	Cortland or Macintosh Apples
¼	cup flour
1	cup sugar
1	tablespoon cinnamon
⅛	teaspoon ground allspice
1	lemon, juiced
1	grated rind of lemon
3	tablespoons butter
1	large egg beaten with 1 tablespoon water

Preheat oven to 375. Peel, core, and slice the apples into a mixing bowl. Mix flour, sugar cinnamon, allSpice, lemon juice, and lemon rind in a bowl. Pour flour mixture over the cut apples. Dot with butter. Add top crust. Make several vents in the top crust. Brush with egg mixture. Sprinkle with 1 tablespoon sugar. Bake 15 minutes at 375, then reduce the temp to 350 and bake 30 minutes longer until the crust is golden brown and filling is bubbling lightly.

Pineapple, Mango and Papaya Squares

2	cups cored, peeled fresh pineapple
1	cup chopped peeled mango
³/₄	cup dark brown sugar
¹/₂	cup orange juice
1	cinnamon stick
¹/₂	teaspoon grated orange peel
¹/₂	teaspoon grated lemon peel
1	pinch of ground cloves
4¹/₄	cups (2½ sticks) unsalted butter, room temperature
³/₄	cup sugar
³/₄	teaspoon vanilla
¹/₄	teaspoon salt
2²/₃	cups flour

Filling

Combine chopped pineapple, mango, papaya, brown sugar, orange juice, cinnamon stick, orange peel, lemon peel, and cloves in a thick saucepan. Cook over low heat until reduced to 1½ cups, stirring frequently. 1½ hours. Remove cinnamon stick. Cool.

Crust

Beat butter, sugar, vanilla, and salt in large bowl. Gradually add flour. Gather dough into ball. Divide in 2 pieces, 1 slightly larger than the other. Flatten. Cover with plastic. Chill 15 minutes.

Preheat oven to 375. Roll out larger dough and transfer it to baking pan. Pour filling into crust. Roll out other dough piece and top the mango mixture with a lattice pattern. Bake for about 50 minutes. Cool completely.

Rum Cake

3	cups all purpose flour
2$^1/_2$	teaspoons baking powder
2$^1/_2$	sticks unsalted butter, room temperature
1$^3/_4$	cups sugar
$^1/_2$	teaspoon salt
5	large eggs
1	cup water
1	teaspoon vanilla extract.

Preheat oven to 350. Butter a 9-inch diameter springform pan with 3–inch-high sides. Whisk flour and baking powder in medium bowl. Beat butter, sugar, and salt in large bowl until light and fluffy, about 4 minutes. Add eggs 1 at a time, beating well after each addition. Mix 1 cup water and vanilla extract in measuring cup. Fold flour mixture into buttery mixture in 3 additions alternately with water mixture. Transfer batter to pan. Bake cake until tester inserted into center comes out clean, about 1 hour. Cool.

Rum Sauce

1	cup packed golden brown sugar
$^1/_2$	cup heavy whipping cream
$^1/_2$	stick unsalted butter
3	tablespoons dark rum
2	tablespoons dark corn syrup
$^3/_4$	teaspoon ground allspice
$^1/_4$	teaspoon ground nutmeg

Combine all ingredients in heavy medium saucepan. Stir over medium heat until sugar dissolves, about 3 minutes. Increase heat to medium-high. Bowl without stirring until sauce is reduced to 1½ cups, about 5 minutes. Cool slightly. Drizzle cake with sauce.

Substitutions

For 1 square unsweetened chocolate, use 3 tablespoons cocoa plus 1 tablespoon butter or margarine

For 1 whole egg, use 2 egg yolks plus 1 tablespoon water

For 2 large eggs, use 3 small eggs

For 1 cup buttermilk or sour milk, use 1 tablespoon white vinegar or lemon juice plus milk to fill cup (let stand 5 minutes)

For 1 cup commercial sour cream, use 1 tablespoon lemon juice plus evaporated milk to equal 1 cup

For 1 cup yogurt, use 1 cup buttermilk or sour cream

For $1/2$ cup butter or margarine, use 7 tablespoons vegetable shortening

For 1 tablespoon cornstarch, use 2 tablespoons all-purpose flour

For 1 teaspoon baking powder, use $1/2$ teaspoon cream of tartar plus $1/4$ teaspoon baking soda

For 1 cup cake flour, use 1 cup all-purpose flour minus 2 tablespoons

For 1 cup self-rising flour, use 1 cup all-purpose flour plus 1 teaspoon baking powder and $1/2$ teaspoon salt

For 1 clove fresh garlic, use 1 teaspoon garlic salt of $1/8$ teaspoon garlic powder

For $1/3$ cup chopped raw onion, use 2 tablespoons instant minced onion

For 1 tablespoon fresh herbs, use 1 teaspoon ground or crushed dry herbs

For 2 teaspoons fresh minced herbs, use $1/2$ teaspoon dried herbs

For 1 pound fresh mushrooms, use 6 ounces canned mushrooms

For 1 cup diced cooked chicken, use 1 can (5 ounces) boned
   chicken
For juice of 1 lemon, use 3 tablespoons bottled juice
For juice of 1 orange, use $1/3$ to $1/2$ cup canned juice
For 1 cup barbeque sauce, use 1 cup ketchup plus 2 tea
   spoons Worcestershire sauce
For 1 tablespoon dry sherry, use 1 tablespoon dry vermouth
For 15 ounce can tomato sauce, use 6 ounce can tomato
   paste plus 1 cup water

A Special Thanks

To my family and friends who always gave me so much love and support. To Brenda Vinson, a wonderful friend who always has a sunny personality and a consistent and everlasting passion for quality. To Jana Autry, my niece, for truly being an artist in print and life. I will always need you! To my sister, Judy Groom, for all the insight into cooking and your great recipes. To Aubrey Jones, for being such a great listener since we were kids. To Winnelle Wise, for being with me from the very start. To Mary Evelyn and Jim Berry, for giving me continued moral support and encouragement. To Sandy McDaniel, for being the most patient employee I have ever had. To my Aunt Opal, for being my close friend and confidant, and for the love you gave me by sharing your stories of the past. To Jorge and Rosita Villa de Mebius, for your international influence in the art of food, travel, and family. To Grace Lewis, for taking such good care of Daddy and all of us for over fifteen years. To the Chester Higgs and the Melvin Bateman familes, for letting me be your "Uncle Donnie."

From the bottom of my heart, thanks to all those special and talented people at Lewis Corner Drug Store of the Cinnamon Basket. To everyone I know and have known who have made us proud, I thank you.

Finally, to Mother and Daddy, who taught us how to respect our past and our future. They continued to impress upon us the importance of knowing who we are, what we believe, and how our future depends on not just our ability, but our willingness to work hard in order to succeed. For my family and the ones to come, we dedicate this cookbook to their memory.

List of Recipes